FOUNDATIONS *of* CHRISTIAN THOUGHT

FOUNDATIONS *of* CHRISTIAN THOUGHT

FAITH, LEARNING, AND THE CHRISTIAN WORLDVIEW

MARK P. COSGROVE

Foundations of Christian Thought: Faith, Learning, and the Christian Worldview

© 2006 by Mark P. Cosgrove

Published by Kregel Publications, a division of Kregel, Inc., P.O. Box 2607, Grand Rapids, MI 49501.

Library of Congress Cataloging-in-Publication Data
Cosgrove, Mark P.
Foundations of Christian thought: faith, learning, and the Christian worldview / by Mark P. Cosgrove.
    p. cm.
  Includes bibliographical references and index.
  1. Christianity—Philosophy. 2. Christianity and other religions. 3. Christianity and culture. I. Title.
BR100.C67 2006
261—dc22   2006019722

ISBN 978-0-8254-2434-2

To my loving and supportive family.
To my beautiful wife, Jo Ann.
To my three sons and daughters-in-law,
Walker and Kirsten, Robert and Julia, and Preston and Jennifer.
You are the important books I must read and into whose lives
I must do my best writing.

Contents

Preface

AFTER EARNING MY PH.D. from Purdue University, I had the rare opportunity to lecture at several dozen state universities on tension points between Christian beliefs and academic thought. That teaching in classrooms on college campuses across the country was as much a learning experience for me as it was an opportunity to introduce my Christian faith into the academic arena. Those challenging classroom contacts convinced me that tensions between Christianity and modern academic thought are not usually at the level of the data of science, psychology, or any other field, but are most often at the level of basic assumptions or beliefs on both sides. My strong interest in integrating faith and learning led me to Taylor University, where for thirty years I have had the chance to teach on the Christian worldview, competing worldviews, and the integration of faith and learning.

These many years of planting faith and learning seeds in student minds have born fruit in the pages of this book. The book begins with the concept of worldview and then examines both faith and learning and the relationship between the two. Five worldviews competing with Christian theism are then surfaced and tested for truth. Five chapters are devoted to naturalism, secular humanism, atheistic existentialism, pantheism, and the New Age movement. Christian theism is then examined and shown to be far better able to explain reality and human nature. Chapters on the evidence for Christian theism, why suffering exists in God's world, and living the Christian worldview in the world close the book.

The ideas in this book are not new; only the manner of presenting them is. I tried to use words and format to image complex ideas. To help make faith and learning ideas approachable for a broad audience, this book has boxed questions and answers to help with understanding the issues. Matrix charts and reader-friendly definitions also lighten the load of grasping the many philosophical and biblical ideas. Credit for the ideas in this book goes not to me but to years of study by the finest of Christian scholars. I chose to reference a minimum number of "well said" quotes, which represent the best tip of the large iceberg of Christian scholarship. By the time readers turn the last page of this book, they should have a well-built foundation for thinking "Christianly" about their lives and culture. The Christian mind is needed in a world that tends to label people of faith as those who have kissed their brains good-bye.

Let the best thoughts come last. I am grateful to my students over the years for interacting with my ideas and offering helpful feedback. I thank Kregel Publications and, particularly, Jim Weaver, Director of Academic and Professional Books; Steve Barclift, Managing Editor; and Jesse Hillman, Marketing Manager. No book is just an author's work. We are all a team in this effort. I was just the one sitting at the keyboard.

Part 1

THE CONCEPT OF WORLDVIEW

Developing a Christian Mind

*Without Christian thinkers much will be left unsaid, for there is no
one else to say it.*

NANCY B. BARCUS

HUMAN BEINGS OUGHT TO live their lives the way we work on large
picture puzzles. With puzzle box in hand, we set up a card table,
dump out a thousand pieces, and take a good look at the picture on
the box. Human life is far more complicated than a thousand-piece
puzzle, but it certainly needs to be lived with a picture in mind of
what life is all about. During some Christmas seasons years ago,
my wife and I and our three young boys worked on large picture
puzzles together. We would begin work on our newly bought, one-
thousand-piece puzzle on the first Sunday of Advent, hoping to
finish the job by Christmas. Whoever wandered through the living
room was supposed to put in a couple of puzzle pieces along the way.
But with small children the puzzle building never worked perfectly,
and we were long into January before the puzzle was finished.

Imagine that one Christmas I bought you an incredibly large
puzzle of ten-thousand pieces. How would you begin? You might
suggest finding the straight-edged pieces and assembling the frame
first. However, the large puzzle I bought you does not have straight

---

Epigraph. Nancy B. Barcus, *Developing a Christian Mind* (Downers Grove, Ill.:
InterVarsity, 1977), 9.

edges; that would make the puzzle too easy. You say, "Turn all the pieces over, colored side up." But, alas, I bought a giant puzzle that is colored on both sides! The huge puzzle does not give you any breaks! To your credit, though, you are giving me subsets of the correct answer.

The best method for building any large puzzle is to know what picture the puzzle eventually makes. The puzzle box top pictures the reality that the puzzle pieces will construct. Pick up an oddly shaped piece of green cardboard from the pile before you. Where do you put it? You can see on the box top that the Grand Canyon picture has blue skies above and green water in the river below. That green piece in your hand must be a part of the river.

This book is about the puzzle of thinking and living our complicated lives and the "box tops" people use to explain themselves and the world around them. I will be calling these box tops "worldviews." Just as puzzles progress best with box tops to help assembly, so too life is lived best when we possess a correct worldview, or picture of reality.

The central purpose of this book is to present the foundational ideas for thinking "Christianly" about reality and life and the "box top," or worldview, that portrays truth. I will stress the word *thinking* when I refer to Christians, because Christians are and must be thinkers. There is nothing about a strong Christian faith that excludes the importance of learning and reason. We must rid ourselves of the notion that faith and learning are somehow opposites or enemies. Some well-meaning Christians think that God is honored by faith alone and is dishonored by evidences or a reasoning mind. However, the human mind is God-created, and we honor God by using our minds and thinking His thoughts after Him.

Christians should be people of faith who can think. All thinking begins with a foundation of faith assumptions. Faith in anything is developed and tested by different areas of the world of learning. Faith and learning are not separate activities but are interwoven with each other for the full functioning of the human mind. In other words, faith is essential for learning, and learning is essential for faith. It is a shame that our current culture at times equates nonthinking with the Christian person. Such an equation should never reflect the reality. Some of the world's greatest thinkers, past and present, have been people of strong religious faith.

The following points summarize the major themes highlighted in this book.

1. Learn to think in terms of worldviews (assumptions about reality and life) as an aid to seeing the relevance of the Christian faith in our world today. Be aware of worldviews other than your own, and know how to test them for truth.

2. Learn to be open to the whole of knowledge, including biblical teaching, the sciences, and the arts, to learn from it and to enjoy it.

3. Trust the firm foundation in the Bible for life and knowledge; upon it Christians can build their living and learning.

4. Learn to integrate faith and learning. The integration of faith and learning shows how one can solve issues between secular and Christian thought. There is nothing helpful today about ignoring the academic tension points between secular and Christian thought. Nor is it usually helpful in Christ-versus-culture issues to merely "proof text" our way to victory using appropriate Bible verses.

5. The Christian worldview is excellent at describing our universe and ourselves and at solving the problems we find ourselves in. Do not think of Christianity as just church attendance. It is both a thoughtful worldview and a personal relationship with the God of the universe. For that reason, studying worldviews, yours and others, is a good way to go about developing the Christian life of the mind.

This book is about the relevance of the Christian faith to our lives, specifically to our intellectual and cultural lives. High school and college students should read this book because their faith is not meant just for church on Sundays but is relevant to everything they are studying in the classroom and to decisions they are making in their culture. Adults should read this book if they are serious about relating their Christianity to modern viewpoints that seem antagonistic to the Christian faith. The Christian faith is a system of thought and behavior, but even more than that, it is a personal relationship with Jesus Christ. We should live out our Christian faith on the foundation of a world and life view that affects all we think and do.

- Part 1 of this book looks at the concept of worldview and the integration of faith and learning.
- Part 2 examines and tests the major worldviews in our culture, including the worldview of Christian theism. People of wisdom know what their worldviews are, and they can test those beliefs. Thinking Christians should be familiar with the popular worldviews embraced by others and know how to test those viewpoints for truth. The major worldviews of naturalism, secular humanism, atheistic existentialism, pantheism, and the New Age movement will be examined and tested in comparison with Christian theism.
- Part 3 explores the Christian worldview in more depth, in order to test it and to show how well it applies to our thinking and living. The Christian worldview is tested in the same way as other worldviews are and found to be admirably supported by many types of evidences.

My own experience with Christianity involved coming to faith years ago during my graduate-student days on a secular college campus. I have since been involved in teaching the Christian worldview at the college level for more than thirty years. Thus I can testify to how well the Christian world and life view relates to the current needs in American thought and culture.

Each chapter makes use of "I Have a Question" boxes that interrupt the text at appropriate points with questions. Some of these questions are used to clarify points that I am making. The boxed questions give me a chance to repeat myself "in other words" without letting the text string endlessly along. Other questions act as challenge questions that do not necessarily agree with the point I am making. Answers will be brief or point ahead to future chapters. Hopefully the arguments in the book are fair to non-Christian viewpoints or differing Christian viewpoints.

I HAVE A QUESTION

Why should I care about any of this? I am living my life just fine. Some people overanalyze everything!

To paraphrase Socrates, "The unexamined life is not worth living." If I could change those words—with apologies to Socrates—I would say that an examined life is much more satisfying and worth living than an unexamined one.

You may feel that life is going well right now, but it will not always be so, for disappointment and suffering enter every life. Just read along and see whether any of these ideas prove helpful to you. And remember, it is a valuable life you are living, and therefore it is worth thinking about.

For ease of learning I will also include a small list of "Some Terms to Think About" at the end of every chapter to help make clear some of the main points or to expand upon some of the ideas. In most cases I will not give precise dictionary definitions for these terms but instead will speak about them with a relaxed familiarity that will add to our understanding of these important topics.

Every chapter begins with a quote that characterizes the chapter or some issue the chapter surfaces. These quotes are from books worth reading, many of them modern-day "classics" that should be on everyone's reading list. These works will be annotated in the "For Further Reading" list at the end of this book. I have kept my citations and reading suggestions to a minimum in the hope that a small number of excellent suggestions might actually attract busy readers into reading more about this book's ideas.

SOME TERMS TO THINK ABOUT

Christian world and life view. A worldview is not just a list of beliefs but a living view; not just an academic endeavor but a personal one as well. Your Christian beliefs are first and foremost personal, affecting not just your mind but all of you and your daily life.

open-mindedness. To be open-minded means to be open to something other than what you already believe. Not one of us is perfect in knowing truth. Therefore, being open-minded to other possibilities for truth is a continuing self-test in your discovery of truth. You can still hold strongly to your beliefs, but you must be humble enough to keep your mind open to other possibilities.

worldview. A worldview is a set of beliefs about reality and human nature. I will give more complete definitions of this important concept in later chapters.

ONE

What Is a Worldview?

*A worldview provides the loom for weaving the tapestry of under-
standing out of the strings of experience.*

ROBERT A. HARRIS

A WORLDVIEW IS A SET OF assumptions or beliefs about reality that
affect how we think and how we live. The important ideas and beliefs that people hold invariably move their thoughts and behaviors.
The young man who believes that he is God's gift to women is going
to act in ways that spring from that egotistical belief, regardless of
what women really think of him. He will, at the very least, be more
self-confident in asking women out on dates. "After all," he says with
a smile, "who wouldn't want to be with me?" And, should he be
spurned, he is less likely than most to interpret those negative results
to mean that women do not like him. He might say that the women
were playing hard to get! He explains, "I could tell when those young
women threw rocks at me and said 'get lost,' that they really desired
me!" He is seeing the world through his own mental "glasses." What
a shame it is for him that his "worldview" does not correspond with
reality, because he is going to get more rocks than dates.

Key beliefs about ultimate reality and personhood always leave
their impressions on daily living. Consider a culture that believes

Epigraph. Robert A. Harris, *The Integration of Faith and Learning: A Worldview
Approach* (Eugene, Ore.: Cascade Books, 2004), 78.

there are no moral absolutes. That culture, much like our own, will exhibit "relativism" in its morals, laws, educational institutions, and political decisions. If you believe that sexual relationships are merely animal activities, then you are not likely to worry much about sexual activity among unmarried teens. Strongly held beliefs lead to specific behaviors and lifestyles. Just as our young man is having trouble getting dates, so too our culture is suffering the consequences of wrong beliefs about reality and life.

Beliefs that people embraced hundreds of years ago can still affect us today. The belief in the value of democracy moved Americans to fight for independence in the Revolutionary War, and it is a belief that most Americans still hold today. It is not just through the pages of books that beliefs travel but also through the fabric of families, education, and cultural habits. Beliefs that arise in one culture may not only affect that culture, but also can drift with the flow of time and affect other cultures generations later. Even great books, past and present, which few read and even fewer understand, can still affect the lifestyles of multitudes. It is to our peril as individuals and cultures that we ignore the major beliefs and ideas that surround us. It is also our loss if we do not know the details and reality of our own Christian worldview. To not know the worldview beliefs of others or to fail to understand our own leaves us unable to defend our Christian faith in an increasingly secular society and a religiously aggressive international scene.

Therefore, it is important to understand this concept of worldview. A worldview is a set of assumptions, or presuppositions, that are generally unconsciously held but affect how we think and live. A worldview is a set of important beliefs that normally we inherit unthinkingly from our academic and cultural ancestors. If you were born in Western culture, you very quickly believed that the world is real, that you can trust your senses, and that you had better be good. You did not develop those beliefs in your first year of college, but as a child you absorbed them from those around you who believed in and acted upon those beliefs. As a teenager perhaps you absorbed new beliefs from your peer group and from television concerning your personal worth, the goals of life, and the morality of sexual expressions.

Beliefs or assumptions affect learning in three ways. First, our beliefs narrow down the subjects we are interested in studying. A person who does not believe in God or the immortal, human soul is not likely to investigate religious conversion or free will as serious options in the study of human behavior. The range of subject matter has been narrowed down by the prior belief system.

Second, our beliefs push us toward certain methods of gathering knowledge. Even scientific investigation can be affected by belief systems. To believe that human beings are just animals may leave us learning about human beings by recording the behavior of rats in cages. To believe only in the physiology of the person can guide us into studying only salivary glands and the senses. Such methods are fine, but by themselves they will limit what we can discover about the person. The findings of science may not be showing us "man the biological machine" as much as the prior assumptions of the scientist are excluding other methods of investigation.

And third, the interpretations an investigator places around the data gathered are controlled by the beliefs the investigator holds. In our studies we come into contact with very few "facts" but with many "interpreted" facts. A Haitian fire walker moves delicately and painlessly across hot coals of fire. There is little knowledge in that observation. What we want is an interpretation of the data: How did he do it? One investigator attributes it to the power of a hypnotic trance. Another sees demon possession. Another sees the pantheistic illusion of the fire. The direction our knowledge takes depends upon our prior beliefs. Needless to say, knowledge gathering, whether in science or religion, proceeds far more accurately when one begins with an accurate worldview.

Worldview Puzzle Building

Perhaps the best way to understand the concept of a worldview and its importance to our thinking and living is to revisit my puzzle example. Imagine again that you have received a ten-thousand-piece picture puzzle as a Christmas gift. You use the picture on the box top as a picture of the reality that the pieces will make when properly assembled. The box top picture is a guide and corrector to you as you undertake the difficult task of arranging the many disordered pieces.

A worldview is like the box top on a puzzle. It is a picture of reality within which the pieces of our knowledge, life experiences, and cultural histories occur. In the midst of a busy, modern life, it is difficult to know the larger meaning of our existence or how moral decisions should be made in our lives. With this puzzle box-top image in mind, you can see that puzzle building without a box top or with the wrong box top would be a severe handicap. Imagine that you discover that a few workers at the puzzle factory switched the box tops on some puzzles. And yours could be one of them! Instead of the Grand Canyon puzzle, which you have been struggling to piece together, you may actually have a Niagara Falls puzzle! Or imagine that you did not get a box top for your puzzle at all because I gave you the pieces of the puzzle in a large plastic bag.

In either scenario you could get started and even make some progress. But it would be tedious and slow at best, and if I kept bringing new pieces every week to add to this ever-expanding puzzle, you would feel the hopelessness of your task. So, too, in a world of increasing knowledge and possible experiences, the complexity and questions about life and happiness are felt keenly. I am not despairing of ever knowing anything by science or our own inner experiences but saying that learning proceeds best with an accurate worldview upon which to build thinking and experience. If one insists that learning can proceed in an academically unbiased fashion without any discussion of "faith" matters, then that person is still operating with an unknown and untested belief system concerning the importance of beliefs to thinking.

People today are not capable of answering the ultimate questions of life and morality based upon their own personal and fragmentary experiences. If I came upon your "box-top"-less puzzle building, I might see you discarding pieces or even cutting pieces with scissors and jamming them into a place in the puzzle that looked half right. Or you might be trying to build a reasonable picture from a small number of pieces. If someone today says that we should avoid the biases of worldviews, especially the religious ones, and just go about putting the scientific pieces together, that person has prejudged the case. All learning and living operates from some sort of box top: worldview beliefs, seen or unseen, examined or unexamined. Wise people realize this and seek to examine and test their own and competing worldviews in order to deal satisfactorily with life's ultimate questions.

I HAVE A QUESTION

I still think that each individual has to find out what kind of life works for him or her. Moral and spiritual matters are personal, private things. We can choose our own box top or design one of our own. Right?

Okay, let's say that your position can be one of the box tops that we are going to examine; that is, the possibility that there are no box tops, that there are no absolute truths that are going to work for everyone. Let's examine many worldview proposals, including that one. But don't get caught saying that it is absolutely true that there are no absolutes in box tops. Let's study a little and find out. In real life you wouldn't say there are no true box tops on how to build safe airplanes or conduct effective heart surgeries, would you? Why be so quick to rule out a true box top for our moral and spiritual lives?

Imagine the difficulty of trying to put together the pieces of a complicated puzzle with no picture to guide you. Your puzzle could become a monstrous, misshapen, and frustrating mess. So it is with our lives and cultures when we try to put the pieces of our lives and culture together with worldviews that are largely incorrect. To say that there is no ultimate truth and that you can choose any worldview you wish or that you can construct any picture you want to out of the puzzle pieces, is a set of unexamined beliefs in itself that should be tested like all other worldviews.

In this book I will start with the idea that it is a good thing to consider the possibility that life is not just described by our whims, but that there is a larger picture of truth within which we must live. Most of us believe in a larger, ordered truth in the academic areas of biology and medicine. Why should it be strange to look for personal, moral, and eternal absolute truths? Who in one's right mind would redefine a cancerous tumor as a growing muscle simply because he or she did not approve of cancer? Your feelings on the matter have no bearing on the true picture of medical reality. You have to deal with reality and find a cure for the very real and harmful disease.

Likewise, why would we expect there to be an undefined reality or worldview concerning our sexuality, personal problems, or moral lives? The wise way to proceed in living and learning is to recognize the strong possibility of and need for an overarching explanation for life and meaning. The next step then would be to examine the major worldviews competing for our attention and to test their evidences for truth and fitness for our living and learning. That examination is what we will undertake in this book. We will look at the beliefs of the major worldviews of naturalism, pantheism, and Christian theism, among others, and test them. We will also see how admirably suited the Christian worldview is to be our foundation of beliefs and how well it fits the evidences we can gather and faces the tests with which we can challenge it.

The Importance of Worldviews

Let's review our definition of a worldview. A worldview is a set of assumptions (or beliefs) about reality, generally unconsciously held, that can affect how we think and how we live. A worldview is a set of presuppositions (to use a similar word) about the nature of the universe in which we live and our place within it. *Presupposition* means "pre-supposing things are this way and not that way." The "pre-," or "before," means we are accepting a view of things before we have a lot of evidence for it. Some things in life are difficult to gather evidence for, and we simply have to start somewhere. A basic presupposition of most people would be, "The world is real." That is, the trees are really there and not just illusions.

It is important to realize that everyone has a worldview. Even scientists, who for good reasons strive for objectivity (to study only what they can sense), admit that they make important ontological (what is reality), epistemological (how we know), anthropological (who I am), and ethical (what is morally right and wrong) assumptions. Some of these assumptions are: knowledge is possible, my senses are reliable, scientists should be honest in their work, and human beings are valuable. When we find ourselves admitting that total objectivity is not possible even in the sciences, we are also admitting that all learning needs the foundation of some core beliefs. The job then is to discover which core beliefs are most accurate.

Faith and learning are always interwoven, even in the natural sciences and in public high schools, which strive so carefully to keep religion a safe distance away. Unsubstantiated biases may destroy the objectivity of our knowledge gathering and should be avoided. But that does not mean that assumptions do not and should not be a part of all types of learning and knowing. Worldviews are essential to thinking and acting. Wise, educated people know the worldview from which they operate, they can test their own worldview for its truth and adequacy for life, and they are willing to learn something about the other major worldviews around them.

I HAVE A QUESTION

What do you say to a teacher who says that our Founding Fathers and the Constitution wanted to separate church and state, and therefore we have to leave all faith matters in our churches and out of our schools?

The Founding Fathers of our country wanted to guarantee that our new government would not establish one religion at the expense of all others. This was to be a land of religious liberty, unlike many of the countries from which our forefathers came. Separating church and state does not mean separating "ideas" and state. No one should be in the classroom baptizing new converts, but why should defensible, Christian ideas about human nature, child rearing, criminal behavior, business ethics, human sexuality, and more be outlawed? The exclusion of Christian academic views on such topics leaves either a vacuum in thought or abandons questions in these areas to unexamined worldview positions.

This book is not about the Christian religion but about the Christian worldview. Christianity is not just a set of rules and religious practices. It is a world and life view, one that we can personally adhere to as well as academically agree with. To defend our faith, we need to show that our worldview is superior rationally, morally, and existentially to any alternative system of belief. Because so many elements of a worldview are philosophical in nature, Christians must know something about philosophy in order to be biblically sound. Christians need to study philosophy and other academic subjects, as well as the Bible. The Bible becomes very important to thinking Christians, not because it is a holy book that can work magic, but because its inspired teachings allow us to develop a cohesive and defensible worldview from which we can speak to any subject or issue that arises in our lives and culture. The Christian faith, therefore, is personal. It speaks of a life lived in relationship with God, in the wholeness of our being—intellect, emotions, and will.

SOME TERMS TO THINK ABOUT

free will. Personal choice that is not simply determined by physical forces. Neither free will nor determinism can be proven scientifically. Reality assumptions in our worldviews turn our heads toward accepting free will or determinism. Therefore, it is important to test our worldview before broadcasting dogmatically in this area.

human desire. It is difficult for any worldview to explain the human desire for truth, beauty, honor, justice, courage, love, heroism, and more. Such desire needs to be *explained* by competing worldviews and not just *explained away*.

ontology. This is a dreadful-sounding word that few of us use in our daily conversations. We could use the word *metaphysics* instead, but that is only slightly better. Ontology refers to the study of ultimate reality and being—what is out there.

presupposition. A pre-belief, a belief held prior to gathering a lot of evidence on the matter. "I *suppose* this is the way things are."

worldview. *Weltanschauung* is the German loanword for worldview: the German *welt* means "world," and *anshauung* means "perception." Even in other countries people are talking about worldviews! I wouldn't ordinarily give you this word, but you will see it in many books.

TWO

Worldview Beliefs and Persons

*[Worldviews are] universes fashioned by words and concepts that
work together to provide a more or less coherent frame of reference
for all thoughts and action.*

JAMES W. SIRE

UNDERSTANDING THE WORLDVIEWS of other people is important
because worldview beliefs are major factors behind cultural and
personal behaviors. A worldview gives us a general picture of all
reality to which we relate our own fragmentary experience and
knowledge. In this sense, a worldview helps organize our lives into
a more meaningful story. It helps us put our daily experiences and
choices into a clearer perspective, just as eyeglasses put the world
into clearer focus for many people. Since worldview beliefs mean so
much to life, it is important to help people understand their worldviews better and why they hold them. We also must help people
improve upon their worldviews when their beliefs have inconsistencies or when their assumptions are not in agreement with good
information. After all, short-term meaning and satisfaction can
come from a belief that eating donuts is the ultimate core of life,
but long-term meaning and satisfaction will come with a more accurate perspective on reality, self, and human purpose.

Epigraph. James W. Sire, *The Universe Next Door,* 3d ed. (Downers Grove, Ill.:
InterVarsity, 1997), 16.

I HAVE A QUESTION

Why do I need all this? This looks way too hard. Nobody should have to think this much. Living is not that hard. Maybe theologians and teachers have to think this way, but not ordinary people.

Don't worry. It's not going to be that hard. But it is good to ask why you need this. Do you remember our definition of a worldview as a set of assumptions about reality? These assumptions are usually unconsciously held beliefs. One problem is that any of us could have learned a way of thinking or acting that is wrong, that does not fit reality, and that will make us unhappy. You could grow up thinking that racial prejudice is okay or that appendicitis attacks are really a product of evil spirits. We live in a world and a culture with many strongly held beliefs that could be incorrect, and we are the ones who suffer if they are.

There are terms and ideas to learn, but after some study you can begin to think according to your chosen worldview without much effort. Even now you are thinking according to some worldview, even if you have not examined it. You might not even know the worldview is there, and yet that worldview system of beliefs can negatively affect your whole life. Remember the guy in chapter 1 who thinks that he is God's gift to women? He needs to test that worldview and change before he gets more rocks thrown at him. He needs to learn how to behave around women, and then he will find himself living in a more pleasant world.

The following chart shows basic beliefs that I will catalogue for the worldviews we will examine in this book. These beliefs often have philosophical labels, which can leave one cold to the whole discussion. But notice that I am using a set of labels that speak to what the particular worldview belief means to daily living. Philosophical ideas are not waste-of-time yawners but ideas that relate to the practical, daily questions and uncertainties of life, even if we give them obtuse labels. The left column states the particular category of belief. The right column lists the issues a worldview speaks to in any particular area of belief.

BELIEFS	THE WORLDVIEW BEING EXAMINED
REALITY (Ontology or Metaphysics)	Is there a God, or many gods, or perhaps different spiritual beings of varying degrees of power? Perhaps there is no God and all reality is just matter. All reality could just be atoms in a temporary arrangement called the universe. Or perhaps this universe of matter is an illusion, and reality is the oneness of an impersonal, universal soul. A worldview may also tell us if there is a reality to existence beyond death.
KNOWLEDGE (Epistemology)	How do we know anything with any degree of certainty? Does my knowledge depend upon sensory experiences alone, i.e., what I can see, hear, taste, touch, and smell? Does knowledge come from my inner experiences, reflections, and reasonings? Is knowledge inborn (innate) or something revealed from heaven to religious groups? Is truth universal, once and for all time, for me and for everyone else?
HUMAN NATURE (Anthropology)	What is a human being? Are we just animals, or are we higher beings? Are we made in the image of God or evolved from ape forms? Are we fallen beings with sin natures? Or are we ascending, sociobiological gene carriers, spreading our reproductive success everywhere? Do we have a spirit or soul that survives the death of the body?
HUMAN PROBLEMS	Why are human beings so beset with problems and unable to live up to their own standards? There is much good in the world of human beings, but there is also much evil. Is the evil due to defective genetics, bad environments, an inherent sin nature, or all three? Why do I have such a difficult time controlling myself? Why am I not completely happy even though I have many things?

BELIEFS	THE WORLDVIEW BEING EXAMINED
SOLUTIONS TO HUMAN PROBLEMS	Is the solution to human problems better genetics, better learning, more religion, or a combination of these? Are acts of violence just normal products of natural development that cannot be avoided?
HUMAN VALUE	Are human beings more valuable than animals? Should individual human life be protected no matter what its form or age? Or, is there only value in humanity as a whole, as a race? Is there no ultimate value in a human being beyond material success or function? Is human value found only in the declared value of existential choices, or evolutionary success?
HUMAN PURPOSE	Is the purpose of human life reproductive success, survival of the fittest, or character development? Or, is there no purpose in a chance world? Is my purpose just part of a larger human group purpose, or is there a purpose for my individual life?
ETHICS	What should be our guide to right and wrong in individual behavior and in the collective behavior of the masses and the nations? Does God reveal commandments and guides for life? Do we follow our impulses and drives, which have guaranteed our biological survival to this point? Is the whole discussion of moral truth a meaningless act, since no ultimate, moral truth exists?
SUFFERING	What is the meaning of the suffering in our individual lives? Is there some larger purpose to human life in the midst of pain? Should pain be avoided at all costs? Is suffering just an illusion? Is the reality of suffering the evidence that there cannot be an all-good, all-powerful God up there watching over us? Is suffering the evidence for an historic original sin, or is it evidence that self is the problem and the end of self is the solution?
MEANING OF LIFE	Is human history just the recounting of the same human behaviors repeated endlessly age after age in a cyclical fashion where nothing means anything and history is going nowhere? Or, is history linear and human lives connected in causal and moral

BELIEFS	THE WORLDVIEW BEING EXAMINED
	relationships? Is there a larger story out there somewhere within which the histories of individuals and nations fit?
HUMAN DESIRE	Is our recognition of and longing for what is true, beautiful, and perfect just an accident? Is our longing for the ideal a hint of a deeper source and purpose for human life? Are all of our artistic productions just surface images of the natural desires for food, sex, and safety?

I HAVE A QUESTION

It seems to me that no one can know for sure which beliefs are correct. That is why they are called "beliefs." So no one can tell me how I should be living my life or what is right and wrong for me. Right?

The concern behind this question is not that there is no ultimate truth out there but that no one can know about religious and moral things with any certainty. This viewpoint is called skepticism, and we will address that issue later in this book. For now let me say that Christianity claims that spiritual truth, at least the basics of it, is not necessarily more difficult than other aspects of life to come to reasonable certainty over, for the simple reason that the spiritual world beyond our own entered our world and left the evidence in an inspired Bible and the life and person of Jesus Christ. It is important to realize that one can gather evidence for those truth claims. But more of that will come in later chapters.

As you can see, there are many questions we have to answer when building a worldview. We need to parade competing worldviews out onto the runway and ask which one answers best the deepest concerns of our minds and hearts. Again, if someone argued that any choice of worldview is okay because these are personal, religious matters, I can only say that decision is itself a worldview belief that says there are no worldviews. The honest, academic approach is to examine the major worldviews, including the one that says there are no ultimate truths, and then test them with agreed-upon tests.

Let us cover one further point about these worldview beliefs. Some presuppositions or beliefs within a worldview, such as reality and knowledge, are more important than others, because beliefs in these areas severely restrict the possible ideas that you can hold in the other belief categories. For example, what you believe about reality narrows down what you can believe about knowledge and human nature if you wish to be logically consistent. If you believe that the universe is nothing but matter, then you have no choice but to believe that human beings, who are a part of the universe, are also mere matter. And knowledge becomes narrowed down to physical, empirical knowledge because there are only physical things and beings to be known. In the same way, your belief about human nature is going to structure your possible answers to human value and purpose questions. For example, if man is mere matter and all matter is determined, then our questions about free will are already answered. There can be no free will unless there is more to man, in spite of any evidence or experience to the contrary.

Therefore, it is important to remember that there are some beliefs about reality and knowledge that are core and far-reaching in our worldview building, and we should take extra care in deciding on these particular beliefs. In fact, it will be very difficult to gather evidence on what ultimate reality is, so we will have to depend in part upon religious views of reality and the existence of God and the evidences for these religious assumptions. Ultimately all worldviews are making some sort of decision on whether God exists, and then each worldview flows out of that initial, often poorly reasoned assumption. In my field of psychology, theories on human nature are just as much or more a product of prior assumptions as they are a product of laboratory research. A wise psychologist should learn to recognize that predisposing assumptions affect what we call truth in psychological or scientific matters.

Before we begin to look at competing worldviews in part 2, chapters 3–6 will examine the questions that have to be answered before one decides on a worldview. These chapters concern the similarities and differences between faith and learning and the testing of worldviews for truth. We will begin by analyzing what faith is (chap. 3) and what learning is (chap. 4). Next, we will look at the different models for how Christians can relate their faith and learning (chap. 5). Then, in chapter 6 we will examine the methods used to test competing worldviews. These chapters are preparing us to think in terms of integrating faith and learning, rather than acting as if faith and learning should be segregated and hostile to one another.

SOME TERMS TO THINK ABOUT

epistemology. The fancy but very common word for ways of knowing. How do I know anything? There are a lot of ways to know things. What would you think of a person who gained knowledge only through dreams? That is not an epistemology for passing algebra or finding a husband. People's epistemologies, or how they gather knowledge, can help or hurt their search for truth.

anthropology. From the Greek word for man, this word means the study of human nature. If I said, "Epistemologies give rise to anthropologies," what does that mouthful of words mean? Think about it. How we find truth (epistemology) can many times limit what we know about human beings (anthropology). If you study only the biology of human beings (epistemology), you are likely to conclude incorrectly that people are merely biological machines (anthropology).

Christian theism. The worldview of Christians. It is a belief in a personal God (theism), and that God is Jesus Christ as described in the Bible. Let it be said up front that not all Christians agree on some of the details of the worldview of Christian theism. Worldview construction is tough work.

THREE

Faith

The Foundation for Learning

*Faith is analogous to the perspective of a world-view . . . in that it
affords a starting point from which to see things whole. . . . Faith
is not close-minded but exploratory; it does not compartmentalize
life but unifies it.*

ARTHUR F. HOLMES

THE CHRISTIAN FAITH IS more than a box top on the puzzle of human living and learning. Faith is a directing picture that moves human mind and life pieces together into a holistic, thinking and behaving person. The question we raise now is how to relate the worlds of faith and learning, specifically how one's Christian beliefs should affect the world of academic learning and culture. I will begin to answer this question in this chapter by describing what faith is and in the next chapter by defining what learning is.

A person's understanding of what faith is and what learning is lays the groundwork for that person's approach to integrating faith and learning. Chapter 5 will cover the different models that people have suggested for relating faith and learning. There is not one single approach to faith and learning integration because Christians are not in agreement on the nature of faith or the nature of learning. My own position on faith and learning integration is that faith

---

Epigraph. Arthur F. Holmes, *All Truth Is God's Truth* (Grand Rapids: Eerdmans, 1977), 73.

needs the world of learning in order to be tested, and that learning and thinking are always dependent upon faith assumptions. Faith and learning should revolve around each other in a continuing, dynamic relationship. They become one, even though our language easily separates the two.

The Christian faith represents a belief system that profoundly affects one's entire life. Thus, faith cannot be separated from ordinary ways of learning or made into a separate, detached, religious learning process. This means that faith cannot be considered an anti-intellectual, spiritual journey to knowing truth but that it is an intellectual and personal journey into areas within and beyond our understanding. Faith should not be considered a separate, unusual form of "otherworldly" knowing that bypasses traditional knowledge but one that participates in all of our normal ways of knowing.

Faith cannot be equated with religious experience, which by itself is not an adequate source of knowledge. Experience is never self-interpreting but must be carefully examined. Religious knowledge for the Christian can come with experience, but the truth of the Christian faith has to stand upon biblical teaching. Biblical revelation claims to be God's act of communicating to us about life from outside the human realm of experience. God took the initiative to communicate with human beings in their language to reveal His nature and ways of relating to humanity. A strong Christian faith is built upon a revelation from God that is public and testable. The Christian faith, therefore, cannot be anti-intellectual.

Can There Be Faith Without Learning?

Answering the question, "Can there be faith without learning?" with a no is not limiting faith or biblical revelation. It is only saying that we human beings are limited in our ability to know spiritual truth. We need to realize with humility that our limitations in knowledge apply to knowing both from the world's store of knowledge and from the Bible. The Bible is inspired and true, but we are not similarly inspired. Without some learning, misleading ideas and gross distortions of the truth can be presented as God's truth.

The most serious problem of faith without learning is that such faith cannot be tested. If faith or biblical knowledge is just believing that God opens my mind to truth regardless of my study, then no one can ever prove my faith to be in error. The religious extremist, who says we should all commit suicide or kill innocent people in the name of God, cannot be shown to be wrong if a sincere faith is the only judge of truth. The extremist's experience of truth may be that God has revealed this knowledge to him in a dream or through his scripture. Without knowledge from another source, this person's faith knowledge cannot be questioned. A certainty in the truthfulness of God's Word will have to come from testing the Bible's truth claims as we would any other truth claim.

To make faith totally a product of private experience and beyond the real world of evidence leaves us with all the potential for error. Imagine a Christian man who approaches a woman and says that God revealed (religious experience) to him that she is to be his wife. What is she to do in the face of his strong faith? She should say to this "religious" man, "Let's check this knowledge of yours with my own reading of Scripture, with the advice of my parents and my pastor, and with a reading of several books on marriage written by Christians." Private revelations from God may occur, but they should always be authenticated by other learning in the form of biblical teaching, the wisdom and counsel of others, and our knowledge of ourselves and the world around us. This is to say that faith can be tested with learning, and God seems to expect us to proceed in religious growth and understanding through growth in relevant knowledge.

I HAVE A QUESTION

If a very religious man in A.D. 1000 became a monk, he would become very spiritual by just doing spiritual things and without studying a lot of the knowledge of the world. Wouldn't it be best today to do the same thing—pull back from the world and concentrate on spiritual things?

First of all, history tells us that monks and monasteries were very often at the center of learning in medieval culture. Second, while a person could concentrate on fasting and prayer in an isolated, monastic life, in our culture today the world of knowledge to which Christians need to be salt and light is far bigger than it was in A.D. 1000.

The Bible's Contribution to Knowledge

The Bible is the source Christians draw from when they look to connect their Christian faith to the educational and life situations around them. Therefore, we must look at what the Bible brings to the table as its contribution to learning. For Christians the integration of faith with learning rests on these two sources of knowledge: the Bible and human, academic subject matter. We need to ask what subject areas these two sources of knowledge address and how helpful and accurate they are in what they discuss. And so we raise two questions: What does faith (Bible) contribute to our understanding of reality, personhood, and personal problems? And, what do the academic subject areas contribute to our understanding of that same reality, personhood, and personal problems?

The Bible is called special revelation from God to distinguish it from general revelation from God in science and the arts. Special revelation refers to God's communication to human beings through the Bible and the person of Jesus Christ. It will be clear in this examination of the biblical contribution to knowledge that I am not attempting to separate sacred, biblical knowledge from secular knowledge in a way that places enormous value in biblical truth and questionable value in learning in the arts and sciences. To do that would be to err by suggesting that biblical knowledge is from God and knowledge from the arts and sciences is not.

Any splitting of knowledge into discrete sacred and secular camps leads easily to the suggestion that biblical knowledge by itself is all we need to know in life. The Bible is important and unique in that it is revelation from the God of the universe, but it still overlaps with other God-given methods in the quest for truth. We must remember that even though the Bible is God's infallible communication to us, we who read it are not infallible in discerning the truth it reveals. Therefore, we need to apply a variety of methods of knowing to the task of understanding our world and also to the understanding and application of the truths of the Bible.

While there are many contributions that the Bible can make to human life and thought, I will mention here only two that relate to the material in this chapter. I am not at this time seeing the biblical contribution to knowledge in terms of the certainty of its knowledge because of its inspiration and inerrancy; I will discuss that topic later. First, the Bible contributes a worldview, which is a set of beliefs or assumptions about reality, human nature, and ultimate, human concerns. These interconnected beliefs provide a guiding and correcting foundation for the pursuit of all knowledge. Second, the Bible also contributes some details of knowledge in many areas of particular importance to human life, such as marriage and family, the human personality, crime and punishment, meaning in life, human sexuality, poverty, anger, and grief, among many others. But it is important to remember that the Bible is not exhaustive truth. This means that while everything in the Bible is true, the Bible does not exhaust all the truth to be known.

I HAVE A QUESTION

Your discussion of what the Bible contributes to knowledge is fine, but it sounds too intellectual—not spiritual enough. Where is the power of God in the Word of God?

That is a good question. There is no "power" in the words of the Bible unless those words are understood and applied in our lives. Maybe the name of Jesus has power in the presence of demons, but other than that the Bible should not be treated like a magical book with words to be recited as incantations in the face of our difficulties. Harry Potter books may talk about magic and spells, but the Bible talks about the power of the truth and truth-filled lives. That truth is not just intellectual but is also mystical in the sense that it deals with this world of the physical in relationship to the world of the spiritual. The deeply spiritual nature of the Word of God is not found in its otherworldliness, but in its revelation of the reality of God and spiritual reality becoming a part of this world of matter and human beings.

The Rational Person of Faith

If I have said anything important in this chapter, it is that a lot of learning and thinking should be a part of the faith development and experience of Christians. One common misconception about faith and religious matters is that you have to kiss your brains good-bye in order to be a religious person. Both religious and secular individuals often hold such a misconception. The atheist often sees religious believers as holding on to outmoded, old-fashioned religious beliefs in spite of plenty of evidence to the contrary. And many Christians become anti-intellectual as they reject the modern theories of Darwin, Freud, and Marx, as well as much entertainment and worldly values.

In this book I want to discuss both faith and learning and the relationship between them, and I want to dismiss the antagonistic approaches from either the faith side or the learning side. I hope it is apparent that faith and learning inhabit similar ground in that faith should always have a learning component, and learning should always be based on faith assumptions. It is not that faith and learning are different forms of the same thing, but they are interrelated. You cannot have a testable faith without learning, and you cannot have meaningful learning without some faith assumptions. Academic and life problems arise when we try to separate faith and learning. Thinking "Christianly" means understanding this relationship between faith and learning. We must always remember that knowledge of the academic sciences and arts is a very important part of the Christian mind and faith in today's world. And thus, to the Christian mind the world is sacred and very much a part of what God wishes us to explore and enjoy.

Modern American culture has been described as post-Christian, meaning that Christian values, which at one time provided a foundation for government, education, and individual behavior, no longer predominate. I am not examining the reasons why our culture has shifted from a sacred to a secular view of reality and life. I am merely pointing out that we are living in a time when faith and learning issues need to be discussed. We are part of a culture that, for the most part, chooses not to relate religious faith to learning or lifestyle but instead suggests that faith matters belong in churches on Sundays, while truth is found in more important experimental or experiential ways during the rest of the week.

One product of living with the habit of separating matters of faith from matters of life and knowledge is our culture's painfully difficult search for guiding values in government, education, and public morality issues. The impeachment of an American president, questions about chastity, abortion, money, meaning in life, respect for authority, the goals of education, the ethical direction of scientific discovery, and more are all issues deeply rooted in the belief systems of a culture.

These problems and challenges, which our news media report on every day, are making many people, Christian and non-Christian alike, propose integrating some core values and beliefs into our living and learning activities. It is to this end that Christians are speaking up about building life and knowledge on the tried and proven core truths of the Christian faith. This is not a plea to superficially add religion to American culture but to state and defend Christian faith assumptions about reality, knowledge, and human persons, and then to live in accordance with those assumptions.

There are two sides to the faith and learning question, and we need to look at both. In this chapter we have examined the nature of faith and its relationship to learning. In the next chapter we will take up the matter of the nature of learning and its relationship to faith assumptions.

SOME TERMS TO THINK ABOUT

exhaustive truth. The sum of all truth. Biblical knowledge does not exhaust all possible truth. There is truth from God that we can discover outside of the Bible—in mathematics and medicine, for example.

faith. Seeing and behaving with a biblical view of reality and human nature. Faith is as much acting in accordance with what we see as with what we cannot see.

faith without learning. Faith isolated from human learning cannot be tested to see whether it is correct. You cannot test every spiritual proposition in the Bible, but you can certainly get a strong feeling for its authenticity from what you can test.

secular knowledge. I do not want to separate knowledge into sacred and secular, so let me not do so here. There is learning from the Bible—sacred; and there is learning from math—secular. But the Bible and 2 + 2 = 4 are both from God, and in that sense both are sacred knowledge.

FOUR

Learning
The Partner of Faith

We do indeed give the primacy to that spiritual truth revealed in the Bible and incarnate in Christ. That does not mean, however, that those aspects of truth discoverable by man in the realm of mathematics, chemistry, or geography, are any whit less God's truth than the truth as it is in Christ.

FRANK E. GAEBELEIN

HUMAN LIVING AND LEARNING does not come exclusively from inherited instincts, controlling genes, or a determining environment. We are free to discover truth and make good decisions, but it is by hard work that this is done. In other words there is no completed puzzle for your life. You have to do the work of fitting the pieces of your life story together. There is indeed a Christian theistic worldview showing you what human life and beyond is all about, but that general picture of life and reality becomes incarnate in your story as you develop from infant to adult. A faith worldview will not by itself give you the details for your thinking and behaving. You are the puzzle with pieces waiting to be put together to form a meaningful and satisfying life.

Learning from academic subject areas, participating in the liberal arts, and the personal experiences of a human being all contribute

Epigraph. Frank E. Gaebelein, *The Pattern of God's Truth* (Chicago: Moody, 1954), 22.

to the development of the person. One's faith worldview provides the guidance and correction along the way. Learning and living in real life give richness and detail to what is a general worldview picture of reality and life. When observed through the lenses of real human life, the faith worldview comes into focus. The pieces of the puzzle of life are far more detailed than the general picture of a faith worldview. And, when learning and experience are added, the elements of the faith worldview stand out and are far better understood. We need human learning as a partner to a faith worldview in order to further develop, understand, and live out that worldview.

When I refer to "learning" in discussing faith and learning, I am thinking of academic knowledge from the sciences and the arts. Christians call this type of learning from human activity "general revelation" as opposed to God's "special revelation" of truth in the Bible. In this chapter we need to see the general contribution of human learning to our questions on reality and human nature as we "flesh out," understand, and apply the Christian worldview.

I HAVE A QUESTION

You mentioned general revelation in academic subject areas and special revelation in the Bible. Doesn't using the word "special" mean that the Bible's knowledge is far more important and superior to human learning?

Yes, biblical knowledge is special and even superior in many areas, but that doesn't mean that human learning in the liberal arts is somehow second best or suspect. The Bible is superior to the learning I can do in terms of discovering spiritual truths, and it is special because it is from God, from outside of me, from the God of the universe who knows these things and wants to reveal them to us. What I read in the Bible about human nature is information from the Creator of my nature, and I can trust that it is true. At the same time, my careless interpretations of the Bible, and my sloppy translation of the Bible from Hebrew and Greek manuscripts, are neither inspired nor special. Human learning, even in nonbiblical areas, is still needed for God's inspired Word to be useful and clear to us.

A fundamental question we are going to have to answer in this book is why God insists on working through human beings when He could do things better by Himself. Suffice it at this point to acknowledge that He does choose to work through our efforts and our intellects. Thus the existence of special revelation from God does not rule out the importance or need for general revelation from God.

Just as we saw in chapter 3 that there are strengths and limitations to faith propositions, so, too, human learning in the arts and sciences has particular strengths and weaknesses. The points below summarize these ideas and give my answers to the following questions about human learning: What can academic subjects teach us, and how accurate or helpful is this knowledge in our search for truth about reality and human nature?

The question of how accurate or helpful human academic knowledge is obviously demands much more investigation than I will give here. Each academic subject area will have to answer this question individually. It is possible that Christians in chemistry might say that the Bible does not speak to the truths of chemistry except in general ways and the human intellect has been fairly good in contributing to truth in chemistry. However, a person studying psychology might feel that the Bible's subject matter overlaps many areas of psychology and that the Bible's contribution is very important. Of course, it is quite possible that human knowledge in psychology is more negatively affected by secular assumptions than human knowledge in chemistry. Thus, human learning may be judged more harshly by Christians in psychology than by Christians in chemistry.

Human learning makes at least two contributions to our questions on reality and human nature. First, the human mind is quite capable of discovering truth. This becomes obvious when we compare life and knowledge in today's world with the world of a hundred years ago. Our great-grandparents would not believe their eyes if they could see our world with its airplanes, computers, cell phones, nuclear bombs, modern medicine, and spacecraft. In spite of two disastrous world wars and much human greed and selfishness, the world has seen a fantastic explosion of knowledge unparalleled in history. To say it simply, even fallen, sinful, human minds can discover much truth about reality and human nature.

Second, all truth is God's truth. This well-known expression means that truth, wherever or however it is discovered, is always from God. Even truth discovered by an atheist is truth from God and, therefore, is important truth for Christians. God as the Creator is the ultimate source of all truth. Therefore, there is something illogical about saying that we do not need secular knowledge because it comes from sinful human beings. Neither the importance of our sacred mission to bring the gospel to the world nor our moral disagreements with secular ideas and behaviors should lead us to reject knowledge acquired through any of the avenues God uses to deliver truth to us. Christians may object to the immoral behavior of a scientist, but the scientist's behavior most often has little bearing on the truth that he or she discovers. Truth is truth.

The human intellect, however, does have its limitations. Limits in human knowledge are due to our limits as finite human beings. But we are also limited in our search for truth by our fallen natures, which can make truth difficult to accept and apply. Knowing truth is not just the product of the intellect but also of the will and the personality. Facts, even scientific facts, do not exist in a polished form waiting to be called truth but only as interpreted facts, the accumulations of observations that are bundled together by our personal and scientific theories. Truth begins not with observation, but with a direction to look and a willingness to see. Sometimes it is difficult for us as fallen human beings to discover truth, particularly about ourselves and the purpose, significance, and morality of life, because the truth can conflict with our own personal or cultural theories in those areas.

Not all subject areas are equally related to the core beliefs of the Christian faith; therefore, not all ideas are equally subject to distortions due to minds running away from the truth. Subject areas like math and the natural sciences, in general, are removed from most central theological beliefs and gather truth well. The social sciences and philosophy are more prone to difficulties in discovering truth. This is because human beings may balk at the truth about themselves and also because it is far more difficult to discover truth in the areas of human nature, society, and ultimate philosophical questions than in the natural sciences.

As I say some critical things about secular, human knowledge, we would all do well to remember that our human limitations and our unwillingness to accept the truth are not only secular problems; they can also affect Christians' abilities to know the truth in the Bible. Bright, spiritual Christians can disagree about the meaning of biblical passages, as our many religious denominations attest. Also, some of the most foolish beliefs exist in the Christian world right alongside sound theology. We would all do well to "learn" how to interpret Scripture and not just wait for the Holy Spirit to blow the cobwebs out of our minds. The Holy Spirit seeks to work through our prepared minds.

Can There Be Learning Without Faith?

Learning never operates without minimal, faith assumptions. All learning must be built on the foundation of some initial and guiding presuppositions. A set of these guiding assumptions is what we have called a worldview. Even the scientist must begin with some basic beliefs, such as: the world is real, communication is possible, I can trust my senses, and the natural laws I discover here are the same throughout the universe.

If one has to learn truth with only the absolute minimum of assumptions, as some have suggested for the natural sciences, then one could investigate only the tiniest of questions about material reality. A scientist could become an expert on hair follicles without importing as many assumptions as required to investigate the causes of juvenile crime. One could become an expert on flea wings with minimal faith assumptions, but one would never be able to answer questions about the ethics of divorce or the existence of life after death without making many more starting assumptions. Such "deep" human questions cannot be studied very well with empirical observation alone and a limited set of starting assumptions. The result of such learning without faith can turn out to be a study of the monumentally trivial, or a study of minute details without connection to other knowledge or holistic pictures of truth. When science does speak beyond the details to larger theories and ethical matters, it is importing a set of assumptions to allow for such conversation. Truly important subjects, even when studied by science, need the grounding and interpreting assumptions of supernaturalism with its "larger than the material world" worldview.

Faith and learning belong together, and knowledge is limited when one is used without the other. Faith needs learning, and learning needs faith. Faith without learning can never be tested for truth, and learning without faith assumptions tends to study the trivial. Christians should strive to integrate faith and learning and thus improve their ability to know truth. This has always been the goal of thoughtful Christians, who have been involved in educational endeavors and the founding of schools from early times.

This use of different avenues of knowledge to arrive at truth (cumulative evidence) underscores the necessity for humility of knowledge. Epistemological (knowing) humility means that we recognize that this world and its people are complex and that we are frail and prone to miss the truth. Therefore, we need to use all the fields of knowledge from the sciences and the arts, guided by a sound foundation of Christian beliefs about reality and human nature, in order to discover truths important for our lives.

Connecting faith development to human, academic learning is sometimes difficult for Christians to accept, because they see it as weakening the concept of faith. A faith that needs development and needs learning is often seen as weak and full of doubts.

However, the truth is that such a faith is "humble," and humility, rather than saying "I doubt," is really saying, "I have much to learn. Teach me." Having a little humility in any learning arena is the key to improving. In practical terms this means that our understanding of the biblical view of the person may be aided by our study of relevant subject areas such as psychology, history, science, and literature. This view resists the tendency of Christians to become dogmatic about their faith. To believe in the dogma (truths we are very certain of) of the Apostles' Creed is to be commended. But to be dogmatic (to make dogma out of ideas about which we are not so certain) has the effect of limiting our ability to learn what God would teach us about ourselves and our world.

I HAVE A QUESTION

I cannot imagine that a biological scientist needs to have religious beliefs in order to do his or her job. In fact, it seems like religion and biology don't need to mix at all. Am I right?

Yours is a good question in today's world of creation-evolution debates. The answer is not simple and demands more details later. For now let's just say that we are not talking about religion and biology but about assumptions and biology. We are talking about whether some biologists are operating with incorrect worldviews that in minor or more serious ways are negatively affecting their abilities to do their science and interpret their results. At the same time, Christians may need to decide with the help of scientific thinking what the biblical content is teaching us about the natural world. There may not be a lot of overlap between biblical content and scientific teaching in biology, but there is some, and we need to do our homework in both biblical interpretation and scientific data interpretation in order to learn more about our world and ourselves. How we do that work will be the subject of the next chapter on integrating faith and learning.

The Role of Learning

The separation of faith and learning produces two major difficulties in the knowledge process. Faith without learning cannot be tested, and learning without faith assumptions tends to produce trivial knowledge. Let us examine these two sides of the faith and learning relationship.

On the faith side, faith without learning never allows you to answer the question of whose faith is correct. Both Muslims and Christians have faith. A Buddhist monk has faith. Mormons have faith. A patient in a mental institution may have faith that he is Jesus Christ. A person may wake up after a frightening dream and believe that the world is going to end tomorrow. All of these individuals have faith, but who is correct? We cannot answer this question if "faith" is the only evidence we are using. Our beliefs need to connect with some other form of evidence by which to test them.

Our beliefs may be true, but the question is how we know they are true. Evidence does not make God's existence true, but evidence can help us to understand the reality of God's existence in the midst of competing atheistic claims. Without some sort of comparative learning process, one cannot know whether his Christian faith is true or just a result of growing up in America. A person who knows by faith alone has no basis to tell the religious crackpot who believes in mass suicide that such faith is misguided. Even biblical knowledge is connected to learning. A good student of the Bible should have knowledge of Greek and Roman history, and some knowledge of grammar and biblical context. Otherwise, Bible verses can be made to say anything someone wishes them to say. Sadly, this is too often the case in the Christian church, as some Christians live out a superficial faith without a solid foundation in learning to support and develop that faith.

The opposite problem is learning without faith. This is learning without allegiance to any particular grounding assumptions. Earlier in this book we saw how this is impossible to carry out. Everyone has worldview assumptions. But many people, particularly in the sciences, argue that aside from a few beginning assumptions, learning should be conducted without any allegiance to religious biases. This is an attempt to be objective in the gathering of all knowledge. It is good to be objective in academic study for this helps us avoid the common biases and misconceptions that people often unthinkingly hold about certain subjects. But to extend this objective purity to the point of rejecting major belief structures for which supporting evidence can be gathered leaves one unable to comment on subjects of any importance.

For topics of any depth, we cannot separate faith from the classroom and expect to fully understand those topics. In the study of ethics, human nature, or ways of knowing, it is clear that faith assumptions are essential to develop those topics sufficiently. But even typical classroom subjects, such as history, biology, and literature are tied to assumptions, which assist in the investigation, interpretation, and application of the material presented in the subject. Assumptions on human nature and the significance of human life are important to knowledge gathering in many subjects.

I HAVE A QUESTION

Isn't there a Bible verse somewhere that says that we should avoid the knowledge of the world?

You may mean 1 Corinthians 3:19, where Paul says, "For the wisdom of this world is foolishness with God" (NRSV). You could have added Romans 1:22, "Claiming to be wise, they became fools" (NRSV). Or Colossians 2:8, "See to it that no one takes you captive with philosophy and empty deceit." Or maybe 1 Corinthians 1:20, "Has not God made foolish the wisdom of the world?" (NIV) Actually, in these passages Paul is referring not to the academic study of history, science, or art but to the refusal of the religious people of his day to see the truth about Christ and His resurrection. The world in all its wisdom would never have chosen the humility of the cross of Christ.

The world's wisdom chooses temporary fame and riches over eternal glory. Paul himself was a great thinker and writer and in no way was banishing the value of a learned mind. However, he did recognize the tendency of a mind in rebellion against God to go astray and see things the way the sinful mind wants to see them. The protection against this type of gone-astray "intellect" is not to become uninformed and anti-intellectual but to reclaim the intellectual and artistic worlds again for God.

Human learning is essential to the strengthening of one's faith. Christian education is taking seriously the notion that one's beliefs affect the academic process and, therefore, it is most intellectually honest to understand and be able to test relevant worldviews, including one's own. Christian colleges rightly integrate faith and learning, meaning their worldview becomes the foundation for engaging in a wholehearted study of the world of knowledge. Christian education, therefore, is not an exercise in propaganda, whereby students are forced to recite Bible verses. Christian education involves a serious study in all of the liberal arts.

SOME TERMS TO THINK ABOUT

"All truth is God's truth." Do not be afraid to study what atheistic or immoral people discover in their searches for truth. The truth is from God no matter who discovers it or what sinful behavior surrounds it.

dogma, dogmatic. Dogma means those truths for which we are so nearly certain that we may bundle them into a creed, rather than keep debating them. The Apostles' Creed is dogma. To put less certain beliefs on the level of dogma is to be dogmatic. It makes sense that not everything we Christians say we believe will be on the level of dogma. We have beliefs about which there is some uncertainty and debate.

empiricism. To know through your senses. Sensory knowledge, or empiricism, is not a problem for Christians. But radical empiricism ought to be a problem for anyone. Radical empiricism says we can learn *only* through our senses. Such a belief is denying the spiritual by prejudging the case.

exhaustive truth. All truth, period. No one person or method exhausts all truth on all subjects. So we should be open to several voices of truth such as the Bible, science, human experience, and philosophical logic. Then our job is determining how to interrelate the various avenues of truth.

humility of knowledge. This is a good way to begin a search for truth: admit what you know and what you are not sure of. Christian dogma does not remove the need for humility of knowledge on the part of Christians.

special revelation. Knowledge that God gives us through the Bible and the person of Jesus Christ.

FIVE

Integration of Faith and Learning

Because ours is one world, religious concepts must make their peace with scientific experience and scientific concepts must make their peace with religious experience. Peace cannot be made by the superficial solution of allocating separate and autonomous realms.

D. ELTON TRUEBLOOD

THE INTEGRATION OF FAITH and learning means the relating of one's biblical worldview to the learning that is taking place in the academic or cultural arenas. Not everyone agrees on how this "relating" is to be done. There are four, very common, general approaches, or models, for the integration of faith and learning, and they are summarized below. Each of these models permits a high view of the Bible as the trustworthy teachings of God. I like the fourth model, a worldview approach, but that does not mean that the others are all wrong. In fact, all of these ways of approaching faith and learning integration have good points for us to consider.[1]

Epigraph. D. Elton Trueblood, *Philosophy of Religion* (Grand Rapids: Baker, 1973), 205.

1. The alternative labels are from John D. Carter's and Bruce Narramore's book to Christian psychologists, *The Integration of Psychology and Theology* (Grand Rapids: Zondervan, 1979). I also recommend H. Richard Niebuhr's classic book, *Christ and Culture* (Grand Rapids: Eerdmans, 1951) and C. S. Evans's *Preserving the Person* (Downers Grove, Ill.: InterVarsity, 1977) for other sets of labels describing faith-and-learning integration models.

There is a strong connection between my preference for an approach to faith and learning integration and the answers I gave to the two questions in the preceding two chapters. Those questions were: What does the Bible contribute to our knowledge about reality and human beings, and what does "secular" learning contribute to those same arenas? I personally have a "high" view of Scripture, a healthy respect for human learning, and a belief that the biblical worldview is a foundation for learning. These beliefs lead me to favor the worldview model of faith and learning.

Sole Authority Model: Faith *Against* Learning

The *sole authority*, or the *against*, model says that faith and learning are antagonistic to one another: faith stands against learning. The Bible is described as the only authority and worthwhile source of knowledge for Christians in the important areas of life. That belief springs in part from the teaching that the human mind is fallen and even bright minds avoid accepting clear truth from God. The sole authority model believes that the Bible is God's trustworthy revelation to us and contains all we need to know to live our lives, share the gospel, and protect ourselves from sinful elements in our cultures. Human learning in the study of human nature and morality is considered nonessential, may be in error, and much of the time is simply not worth the effort.

One positive thing about the sole authority model is that it recognizes that there is much in the world of learning and culture that is wrong or even anti-Christian in its bias. One negative effect of this model is that it tends to shut one of the two "books" of God's revelation to us. The extreme "against" models find themselves at odds with historic Christianity's two-book approach to knowledge. The two-book approach says that God communicates with us through both special and general revelation. Special revelation is God's communication to us through the Bible and the person of Jesus Christ. General revelation represents knowledge from the world of literature and science and indeed all of human learning and experience. In fairness it must be said that whatever approach we take to integrating our faith with learning and culture, we are going to find ourselves against some things in the modern secular culture. But in terms of our witness to the world and our understanding of our own faith, it seems disabling to be against everything in culture and learning.

Separate Authorities Model: Faith *and* Learning

The *separate authority*, or the *parallels*, model of the integration of faith and learning says that faith and learning are not enemies but are complementary sources of truth. God expects us to learn about spiritual things from the Bible and about the things of the world from the academic disciplines. The term *parallel* refers to the idea that these two sources of truth, like the two rails of a train track, run parallel to one another. They are both needed, but they do not cross or overlap into each other's territory. On Sunday you can learn spiritual truth in church about your spiritual life, and on Monday through Saturday you can learn the world's truths in the classroom.

The parallels model seems to work best in the natural sciences, where there is less overlap with the subject areas of the Bible. The Bible contains no chemistry, therefore, we learn chemistry from our class textbooks. However, to say that there is *no* overlap between academic subject areas and biblical truth is to ignore areas of obvious overlap. On the subject of human nature the Bible has much to say about child rearing, crime and punishment, sexuality, marriage, poverty, anger, jealousy, meaning in life, and more. It is clear that the Bible and human academic pursuits are not always parallel but may often overlap. In these cases we have to deal with the conflicts that will invariably arise.

Equal Authorities Model: Faith *Plus* Learning

The *equal authorities*, or the *integrates*, model admits that there is overlap between the content of the Bible and the content of academic subject areas. This model says that faith and learning correlate with one another. The Bible and human subject areas are equal sources of truth, and we should combine them to produce more truth than if we had used either alone. Each source of truth, special and general, contributes to our understanding of certain topics— human nature or ethics, for instance.

In favor of this model is the fact that it accepts both special and general revelation. However, problems arise from the idea of mixing these two very different forms of truth. When we look at the Bible, we do not see many details of knowledge as we do in the sciences or the social sciences. There are some details on human nature but not many. Human learning on the other hand is filled with details of knowledge in millions of books and journal articles. The mixing of a few Bible verses with a multitude of secular journal articles often results in a product that is very secular because we are looking to the Bible only for details in certain subject areas. And where the Bible is silent, as it is with many academic subjects, secular knowledge goes unquestioned. A better approach is to recognize that the Bible contributes a different form of truth in addition to its details, a form excellent for building the Christian philosophical worldview from which the academic subject areas can be evaluated. That brings us to the worldview model I will use in this book.

Foundational Authority Model: Faith *Supports* Learning

The *foundational authority*, or the *worldview*, model says that the major contribution of the Bible to our academic and life pursuits is that it gives us a worldview foundation from which to do our studies in science, social science, and the arts. This worldview approach acknowledges that beliefs do make a difference in academic pursuits. One's faith or worldview does matter when one engages in the learning process. Our beliefs affect: (1) the subject areas we take an interest in studying, (2) the methods we use to study anything, and (3) the interpretations of, or meaning we bring to, the accumulations of facts. In other words, the learning process in school is never an academically unbiased process; one's learning is always affected by one's worldview beliefs. The worldview model, therefore, seeks to transform culture and ideas rather than reject, ignore, or just mix with culture and ideas.

I HAVE A QUESTION

These models are all pretty confusing. How do I decide what model I want to pick, and what difference does it make anyway?

I appreciate your question because at times it gets pretty confusing for me also. The models of integration go back to the two questions we were asking in previous chapters. (1) What do you think the Bible contributes to our knowledge, and how important and accurate is it? (2) What do you think human learning contributes to our knowledge, and how important and accurate is it?

The sole authority, or "against," model has a "high" view of the Bible and a much lower view of the human intellect.

The separate authority, or "parallels," model sees great value in both the Bible and academic subjects but says they do not deal with the same areas of responsibility. In other words, there is no need to integrate or relate faith and learning. Biblical truth belongs in church, not in schools.

The equal authorities, or "integrates," model says that both the Bible and human academics contribute much knowledge to us. These two sources of truth are from the same God and should be saying the same things to us, even if in different words. You just have to combine both sources of knowledge, and you will have more knowledge than with either one alone.

The foundational authority, or "worldview," model is similar to the equal authorities model except that this model says that the Bible does not merely contribute details of knowledge in some subject areas. Rather, the Bible's primary contribution to knowledge is that it gives us the Christian worldview as the foundation of faith from which all the academic subjects are studied. In the Christian worldview, our beliefs affect how we think about and apply the subject matter we are studying. I like the worldview model because it says that a biblical mind-set should guide all that we do and study. And, the worldview model wants us to heartily engage the world of academics and the arts.

There are several ways that a good integration model for faith and learning, such as the worldview model, can be of help to us. Three of those ways will be discussed below: (1) integration of faith and learning can give us a filter on our thinking, (2) integration can change us and our thought patterns and thus change how we learn and interpret information, and (3) integration produces a two-way growth process between faith and learning.

Integration Can Offer a Filter for Our Thinking

The Christian worldview can act as a filter to help us evaluate the subject matter we are studying. The Christian worldview provides a list of truths that we can use to check the interpretations and theories of the ideas we are studying. For example, when a social scientist says that human beings are innately good, we know that this cannot be completely correct. This is because the Christian worldview says that human nature is fallen in spite of its many good points.

The filter function in the integration of faith and learning process, where faith acts as a filter for learning, is helpful, but it has its limits if this is all that our model of integration does. The Christian worldview can act as a filter to screen out erroneous ideas, but the Christian worldview is a limited set of beliefs, most of which are very general. The Christian worldview does not contain very specific beliefs that would allow us to pass judgment on some of the data or applications in many academic subjects. For example, the

Christian worldview will not speak directly to the models of brain function, human memory, or for which political party to vote.

A limitation to using the filter approach as our entire approach to integration is that a Christian's knowledge will only be as helpful and enriching as what is present in the secular mind and culture. If the Christian thinker merely cuts out the bad and keeps the good of secular thought, then his or her knowledge will never have any novel insights or interpretations arising from a uniquely Christian approach to thought and life. A second problem is that not all Christians believe the same things, even though they are all studying the same Bible. In other words, Christians are not always correct as they interpret the meaning of certain biblical passages and attempt to apply them as filters to cultural issues and practices.

Integration Can Change Us and How We Think

The Christian worldview is not a static creed that we memorize but a living belief system that we enter into with our whole lives. Christianity is a living relationship with our Creator. This relationship affects us in ways that can change how we function as scholars, musicians, politicians, and parents. Christian maturation can relate to the work of a person in various ways. The Christian who is growing in Christlike compassion might spend more time and resources in the study of the family or of alcoholism, rather than in academic or cultural areas more current in the mind of the world. This does not mean that a Christian cannot enter fields of study and work of their own or of current world interests, but that often the Christian's efforts will be directed along other lines unique to the Christian mission in the individual and the world.

The Christian worldview might so greatly change one's view of reality and of human nature that Christians would develop new ways of seeing things. A Christian might, for example, be more inclined to see the benefit of preventive styles of counseling. Christians know that immorality can result in social and psychological problems.

Instead of just counseling the juvenile delinquent, the Christian counselor, with God's view of family life, might focus his or her efforts on preventing delinquency by strengthening family structures. Such an approach reflects a different kind of thinking because of one's Christian worldview.

Integration Is a Two-Way Growth Process

"Two-way" means that a good integration model allows for the fact that faith should affect learning *and* that learning should affect faith. We have already mentioned two ways that faith affects learning. Faith can be our worldview filter to help us choose what is correct or incorrect in thinking and acting. Faith also can change us and how we think so that we develop new and better ways of thinking in the academic disciplines. But it is also true that learning can affect the development of our Christian faith.

When I say that learning can affect faith, I am saying that our faith is not an unchanging creed that we rigidly adhere to. Yes, our faith does have dogma, beliefs that we all agree are true, such as those in the Apostles' Creed. But a better understanding of faith is to think of it as a process of developing a mind and heart tuned to God and His truth. We do not know how to interpret every verse in the Bible when we are in elementary school. But with study and good teaching, we "grow" into many of our beliefs as we learn and mature. Some of the learning that affects our faith development comes from Bible teaching, but some also can come from more ordinary learning. Knowledge of grammar, logic, history, and current events often makes Scripture come alive for us. General knowledge in astronomy makes Psalm 19 more meaningful to us. One who has aged or suffered is often able to learn more from the wisdom of Ecclesiastes than one who has never faced tragedies in life.

I HAVE A QUESTION

Your last point that faith and learning integration is a two-way growth process sounds good, but there has to be some limit or some percentage of contribution from important biblical teachings when compared to the contributions of Freud or Darwin or worse. Am I wrong?

No, you are not wrong as long as you do not want to make the contributions of the arts and sciences a zero. Yes, for most subjects of importance, the Bible is preeminent. But do not expect the Bible to teach you all the knowledge you need in the modern world. This point is not about the relative contributions of Freud and the biblical book of Romans, as much as it is about the interaction of spiritual growth and biblical understanding with those ideas you are learning in school or life experiences. The question becomes, Can you fully understand the Bible without some knowledge from history, geography, psychology, and other areas?

Biblical understanding and spiritual maturation do not happen in a vacuum. There is a constant interplay between your faith assumptions helping you engage and process academic learning and the learned and living ingredients that more fully develop your faith. A fourth grader can read the Apostles' Creed or Psalm 51. But the older, more experienced, more widely read Christian can have the theology and commitment of Psalm 51 as a part of his or her being. Faith and learning seem to weave a person of faith. And no, I would not put equal weight on Freud and inspired biblical truth. However, medical texts would make more contributions than any biblical passage in my study to be a medical doctor.

SOME TERMS TO THINK ABOUT

equal authorities model. "I have two sources of truth in the study of reality and human nature: the Bible and the human academic world. I just combine their insights when I have questions, and then I have more knowledge than anyone who uses just one of these God-given sources of truth. A Christian college would be an advantage to me as I study both Bible and academic subjects."

foundational authority model. "My biblical knowledge and Christian life have changed me so that I think in different ways now when I study in areas such as history, psychology, or literature. Calculus is pretty much the same, but I see so many things differently now in other areas of study. A Christian college is helpful to me if it teaches the Christian worldview as a foundation for thinking in all the academic disciplines."

separate authorities model. "I read the Bible for my spiritual growth, but I don't know why anyone would expect to find principles of biology and psychology there. There is no Christian chemistry. There is no Christian psychology or Christian physics. I think a state university is a fine place to earn a college degree, and I will certainly attend a good church there."

sole authority model. "I don't need anything but the Bible to prepare me for life. Why should I harm my mind with the errors of the world? What I need are Bible courses that will prepare me for ministry to a lost world. A Bible college would be a good place to study."

SIX

Testing Worldviews

For entirely too many Christians, reason is seen somehow as an en-
emy of the Christian faith. I disagree strongly with that widely held
but self-destructive thesis.

RONALD H. NASH

THE WORLDVIEW WE HOLD should not be a matter of personal preference. We must test our beliefs with evidence and logic. In puzzle
making there is every reason to believe that we have the correct
box-top picture on the puzzle we buy, unless there have been some
disgruntled workers in the puzzle factory. If our puzzle had the
wrong box top, that would create headaches and wasted puzzle-
building time. We would discover the problem and then get the
correct puzzle picture or go on to some other puzzle. Life, however,
is more complicated and more precious to us than puzzles. There
are competing box tops claiming to have ultimate answers about
purpose in life, moral decisions, and the route to fulfillment. Since
different worldviews are being proposed all around us, we need to
know whether we have the accurate picture of reality as we build
our lives.

To say that there is no one "box top," or worldview, is a box top
in itself, or a relativistic worldview. We can test that claim as well

---

Epigraph. Ronald H. Nash, *Worldviews in Conflict* (Grand Rapids: Zondervan,
1992), 55.

by seeing whether any box top or worldview claim really does have worthwhile evidence supporting it. To say it is just too difficult to figure out the box top for life building, so we should just do what we want in this hopeless situation, is skepticism. Skepticism too is a worldview belief. We can test it and show that, while the ultimate questions in life may be difficult to answer, it is not impossible to draw sound conclusions from the evidences we gather.

In raising this subject of testing worldviews, we must not immediately think that the Christian worldview should not be tested or that it is somehow unspiritual to look for evidences for what we believe as Christians. All worldviews need testing through the world of learning. The ultimate questions of life may be beyond purely empirical study, but that does not mean that faith matters should be removed from the world of thinking and learning. Faith without learning ends up unquestioned, and as a result anyone's faith becomes okay, and truth in faith matters becomes relative to each individual. In developing and testing a worldview, we must admit with humility that we have a limited ability to know about some things with a high degree of certainty, but let us not become skeptics about this business of holding some beliefs confidently.

I HAVE A QUESTION

Isn't it an insult to God to try to test our faith worldviews? Faith is believing, not doubting. And real faith happens when you don't have any special evidence other than the Word of God.

This is a good question to ask because a lot of Christians may feel this way. There is a difference between doubting God and being uncertain. There is nothing wrong with not knowing everything in life or in the Bible. Doubt refers more to not going along with what you know to be true. To ask who wrote the epistle to the Hebrews, or whether the charismatic gift of speaking in tongues is appropriate today, or whether women can become pastors are not questions asked by people of little faith. To not know what a biblical passage means is not the sin of doubt. Uncertainty in biblical matters represents humility and a posture of being open to learn more from God and the Bible. A person may step ahead in faith, even though there is still some uncertainty about how to practice some Christian living principle. A person with uncertainty should read books and commentaries on the question and ask the advice of a pastor in order to come to a greater understanding of what he should believe.

Here are the major tests of a worldview. We will use them on the worldviews we examine in the second part of this book.

The Test of Evidence

Does the worldview fit the facts we can discover about the world? This is the test of evidence. Is there any evidence to support what I claim to be true? For example, I believe that there is much in the way of evidence that suggests that human beings are more than mere biological machines. The test of evidence includes scientific and experiential, or "life," evidences. A worldview should be relevant to what we already know about the world and ourselves.

The Test of Logical Consistency

This test asks whether every belief in the worldview agrees with every other belief in the worldview. Why should we accept an inconsistent worldview—one that holds contradicting beliefs? I find it difficult to believe in any worldview that says that the universe is just a determined machine with no Creator, but that we human beings are special persons with meaning and freedom to our lives. Those two beliefs should not be held together, unless we do not mind being inconsistent in our beliefs. This test is sometimes called the test of intellectual coherence or the test of reason. This is a test for contradictions in the worldview, and contradictions spell doom for a belief system, especially if the contradictions are at the heart of the system.

The Test of Existential Repugnance

This test asks whether it is possible to live the worldview in the world as we know it. This is not a test of whether one is able to live up to the requirements of his or her worldview. I cannot live the perfect Christian life, but I can imagine a world in which it is desirable to live in accordance with the teachings of Christ. If you cannot conceive of your belief about human nature being lived out in real life, then why do you believe it? Many people say they believe in determinism, that human choice plays no part in shaping individual lives or the events of history. It seems existentially repugnant, though, to live one's life with such a paralyzing belief. Sometimes this test is called the test of practice in the laboratory of life. Can you even imagine human beings living in the way that your worldview suggests?

What if someone—a pantheist, for example—rejected these tests of a worldview as too Western or too Aristotelian? What if you did not believe in the physical world or its evidences as real, or if you believed that illogic, not logic was the only rule? In other words what if you rejected the law of noncontradiction (a thing and its opposite cannot both be true: it cannot be both raining and not raining)? The test of existential repugnance is a powerful test to help answer these objections, because everyone on the planet, including pantheists, seems to live as if the world is real, as if communication is possible, as if our senses can be trusted, as if logic and morality are important. Everyone gets out of the way of New York City buses, eats food when hungry, and rejects some kind of immoral behavior. This test, like the first two, comes from how people everywhere and for all time seem impelled to live their lives. Therefore, it seems reasonable to test all the worldviews we study with these three tests.

Human Nature as the Best Test of a Worldview

We ought to test every worldview very carefully in the light of the marvelous evidence of the human personality. Atheistic worldviews find it no challenge to explain rocks and toads with only atheistic and materialistic underpinnings. What is far more difficult for any worldview to explain, however, is the existence of personal beings in an impersonal universe. Personality, in the sense that I am using it, refers to self-awareness, symbolic consciousness, free will, moral notions, creativity, and spiritual aspirations.

To argue against personhood in human nature is to argue, not from experimental evidences (and certainly not literary and religious ones), but from materialistic assumptions. The evidence is before us in complex human behaviors and in our own personal experiences and must be reckoned with. Human beings are conscious and self-conscious in ways that are not limited to sensory input. Human beings possess symbolic existence through language, math, and art. Human beings long for truth, beauty, virtue, and eternity, and have brains (assumed to be the most complicated physical structure in the universe) built primarily to serve these functions.

Christian theism claims that a personal God is the creative source of the human personality. The best that atheism can do is to dismiss the human personality with comparisons to primates or fossil man or to claim that the personality attributes are there but are freakish products of evolution, accidental progress stories for the moment.

Every worldview needs to explain what is so apparent to human beings, and that is the inner human world of symbolic thought, self-reflection, and complex emotion and motivation. These are the elements of mind that propel our individual behaviors. The efforts of atheistic naturalism are directed more to explaining away rather than explaining these things, as we will investigate later. We see this, for example, when human language, religion, art, self-awareness, moral notions, and more are said to be just larger, quantitative versions of primate abilities.

We see this reductionism in the naturalistic tendency to explain away human personality with evolutionary, biological explanations for the complexities of human nature. Mind exists, say many evolutionary biologists, but it is of no consequence in human behavior. Thoughts, desires, and decisions merely tag along after the fact of behavior, propelled by millions of years of evolutionary crafting of human beings for reproductive success. All literature, all art, all compassion, all romance, all searches for truth and beauty are lost in naturalistic, reductionistic assumptions. It is not experimental evidence we must argue against, but presupposition against the overwhelming personal and public picture of human thought and behavior.

Unlike atheistic naturalists, atheistic existentialists, whose worldview we will study later, admit to the uniqueness of the human personality. However, they say that with no more source in the universe than material beginnings, these personality characteristics of human beings are just freakish products of evolution. The personality products of self-awareness, free will, language, and moral sensibilities have evolved to no purpose in a material universe, or at best they hang on because of some small contributions to reproductive success.

We will see in a later chapter that pantheism as a worldview fairs no better than atheism in explaining the human personality. Atheistic naturalism explains away human nature by reducing man to mere nature. Pantheism explains away human nature by raising all of nature, including human beings, to the "universal spirit" level of existence. To the pantheist, human nature is not distinct from the rest of nature. In fact, to the philosophical pantheist, human nature does not even exist except as illusory perceptions to be discarded in meditative or biofeedback sessions. Human personality is not explained but is explained away.

What is needed is a worldview that can explain our self-awareness, our deep desires, our feelings of freedom, and our moral and spiritual motivations. These mental states are not common experiences operating among the many life-forms on the planet;

they are the unique experiences of the dominant creature on the globe (using any sensible definition of dominance). The legacy of human achievement over the past five thousand years is enormous, and the last hundred years have been no less than staggering. It is no explanation to say that human beings are just naked apes or freak products of evolution. I am not arguing against evolution in saying this but arguing for an investigation and explanation for the human personality. Christian theism suggests that it is a personal God who is the source for the personal in man. Since man was created a part of the material world, we should expect our connection with the forces of nature to be strong, but we also should expect to see our unique personal existence making its connections to the personal and spiritual life for which we were created.

I HAVE A QUESTION

I know you said something about this before, but it does seem like you have stacked the deck of evidence against viewpoints like pantheism, which don't believe in logic or see the world and its evidence as illusion. What do you say to a pantheist who argues that illogic is the only test of reality and those experimental reports don't really exist?

I don't mind answering this again. Have we Christians just picked the tests we wanted so that Christianity passes the tests and we can announce that we have won the battle against other worldviews? Actually, it is not that way at all. These tests of evidence and logic are based on how human beings, including pantheists, have lived and tested their world for truth for thousands of years. The third test of a worldview is existential repugnance. Can you live as if these beliefs are true? Can anyone live as if the world is not real or as if illogic is the only framing scheme for life? The answer is no. All people, everywhere, for all time live as if they trust their senses, and they, pantheists included, accept sensory evidence every day of their lives. They walk through doorways and communicate with other people just like everyone else. In other words, even though the pantheist says he believes reality is an illusion, he still lives as if the world is real and that his senses can be trusted. These tests are not just Western or Christian or Aristotelian. They are based on how most people most of the time have and do test reality. So, let's use them.

SOME TERMS TO THINK ABOUT

evidence (test of). Is your worldview in agreement with scientific and experiential observations? Does the worldview fit the world?

existential repugnance (test of). Something fights (Latin *pugno*) against your inner being to live (existential) a certain way. If the world is just an illusion, as pantheists say, then why do they swat flies and eat hamburgers just like everyone else? And the true pantheist, who does not believe in the sensory world, unfortunately will die if struck by an "illusory" falling tree!

logical consistency (test of). Does every belief in a worldview agree with every other belief in that worldview? You do not want one belief in a worldview to say one thing and another belief in the same worldview to contradict it. "All the universe is matter, and I am a part of the universe, but I am not mere matter," the secular humanist says illogically.

Part 2

WORLDVIEWS IN CONFLICT

Modernism and Postmodernism

In the modern period the center of gravity shifted from God to man, from Scripture to science, from revelation to reason in the confidence that human beings, beginning with themselves and their own methods of knowing, could gain an understanding of the world. . . . In the postmodern period, confidence in humanity as an objective, omnicompetent knower has been smashed.

DAVID K. NAUGLE

CHRISTIAN THEISM WAS THE worldview that guided the education, politics, and personal lives of most of Europe until the end of the seventeenth century. Many historians believe that the Christian worldview was the major source of fuel behind the phenomenal explosion of scientific interest in Europe from the 1600s on. Some tend to overemphasize the trial of Galileo by the church in 1633 and argue that faith was a major impediment to the rise of science. But Galileo's trial was not about real biblical faith but about unwarranted faith in the Greek classics adopted by the church and about the politics of being in charge. The Christian worldview gave a theological foundation that undergirded the fledgling scientific

---

Epigraph. David K. Naugle, *Worldview: The History of a Concept* (Grand Rapids: Eerdmans, 2002), 173–74.

enterprise. That foundation included the ideas that God created an orderly world and the minds of human beings and that He gave a charge to all humankind to exercise stewardship over that world and thus draw closer to one's Creator. There was confidence in the human mind because God would not play tricks on His creatures but expected them to think His thoughts after Him.

The Christian worldview is certainly not the foundation for thinking today in most European or American academic institutions. In a span of less than two hundred years, the guiding worldview in academics and learning shifted from theism and a belief in a creator God first to deism, belief in a God who created and then abandoned the world, leaving behind no signs of Himself, and then to naturalism, the belief that there is no God.

In academic institutions the doctorate most often pursued is the Ph.D., the Doctor of Philosophy. Ph.D. degrees abound even though few college instructors even study philosophy. They study history, biology, chemistry, psychology, literature, and more, and all those disciplines can award the Ph.D. degree. The reason for this designation for advanced degrees is that at one time, during unifying theistic days in Europe, everyone studied upon the foundation of the Christian philosophical worldview. This meant that the ultimate questions about God, man, purpose, and ethics were to be answered by all the disciplines, from the arts through the sciences. Hence, all scholars were studying the ultimate philosophical questions in their respective disciplines under the umbrella of the Christian philosophical worldview. But when the Christian worldview was supplanted by deism and then naturalism, the disciplines were left adrift. With no ultimate worldview, all that was left to study were the details of the disciplines with no certainty of putting all things together into one truth.

The word *university* comes from two Latin words *(uni-veritas)*, meaning "one" and "truth." The university originally was a place of learning on the foundation of one truth, the Christian worldview. After the passing of Christian theism, the word *multiversity* seems much more appropriate. But no one suggested changing the general name of the learning institution or the highest degree awarded.

While we have not dumped the label Ph.D., if you look at most Ph.D. dissertation titles, they concern the tiniest of details—all that is left to study are increasingly large and unassembled catalogues of facts that often become college textbooks. College used to be interesting, but now we struggle to keep up with the puzzle pieces of knowledge and to explain to our students why all these facts are important. And if teachers do explain with larger pictures of reality, the theories are limited to each isolated discipline.

The result of this slip from theism to atheism (naturalism) is a culture that has mentally and behaviorally cut anchor and now floats adrift. This shift of worldview represents a shift from premodern thinking to modern scientific thinking, which acts as if the religious beginnings of science do not exist. And now, even modernism and its worldviews have been challenged in another shift to postmodern thought and its worldview alternatives.

This introductory chapter is not about two worldviews competing with Christian theism but about the general, background thoughts that give rise to specific worldviews. In this sense, modern thinking and postmodern thinking are the "wallpaper" in the room called a worldview. They are the soil of a culture or an individual's mind-set. Modernism and postmodernism represent the unspoken, undefended "feel" of what reality is all about. Modernism and postmodernism are "*zeitgeists*," or spirits of the times. They represent the direction of culture, which is leaning away from traditional belief in God and toward the cold, empty world of atheism or the spirit-charged worldviews that take many forms.

Modernism

The term *modernism* refers to modern thought. It is associated with a time period in history when people began to think in more "modern" ways, leaving the myths and legends and sometimes religions behind in favor of scientific and rational thinking on life. Some say the modern age began during the humanistic Renaissance with the flowering of scientific thought around 1600 c.e.

I HAVE A QUESTION

What's C.E.?

You are very observant! I normally use A.D. for dates after Christ's birth. A.D. comes from Anno Domini, "the year of our Lord." Some people in this modern era object to tying everything to Christianity and recommend that we use B.C.E., "before the Christian era," and C.E., "the Christian era." It's not much of a difference, but it shows how much our cultural thinking has changed. Personally, I still prefer to say and write "A.D." But I just wanted to make a point to help you sense the spirit of changes that can come with modernism replacing Christian theism.

The development of scientific progress, beginning in the 1600s with the rise of serious study in physics, chemistry, and biology, has been seen as the foundation for our life in the modern age. That period of scientific discovery was not at all cut off from a Christian view of reality and God's creative order in the universe, but over time there was a loss of faith as the modern age developed. The humanistic Renaissance, beginning with a flowering of human art (1200s), was followed by what is called the Enlightenment, when the Christian foundation for human expression began to be ignored. Then the rise of the sciences in the 1600s opened up the possibility of thinking of the world without God. By the time Charles Darwin's *Origin of Species* was published in 1859, there was a decided gap between some scientists and religious leaders.

The modern age has come to stand for the agnosticism—or atheism, or naturalism— and relativism behind much of today's decision making. Some people say the most significant development of the modern age is the rapid rise of science since 1945 and the end of World War II. Since that time there has been an explosion of knowledge in medicine, transportation, war machinery, electronic communication, computers, and space exploration. This change has been accompanied by rapid lifestyle changes and a growing secularism in the West. As such, *modernism* has not been a popular word for Christians. The danger for Christians, though, is that along with rejecting the atheistic views and behavior of a modern culture, they might also reject the knowledge and progress of that culture. As we will see later, modernism was a spirit of a whole age, a way of thinking, and it is still strongly with us today. However, the end result of modernistic views like the naturalistic worldview has been a demeaning of humankind. We will look later at crises in knowledge (epistemology) and understanding of human nature (anthropology) that arise simply because a personal God and personhood in human nature have been removed as options. The result has been a depersonalizing worldview in naturalism that is very difficult to translate into real life from the pages of the philosophy books. Therefore, a rumbling of changes began to occur in the 1950s and 1960s that were intended to bring the personal back into guiding worldview systems and avoid the dead-end crises of naturalism.

Postmodernism

The word *postmodernism* almost defines itself by saying it is that which comes after modern thought. Modernism, or modern thought, beginning about the seventeenth century and continuing until today, can be distinguished from the Christian theistic worldview, which came before it, and postmodernism, which came after. The newer views of reality and knowledge have not completely replaced the older ones. They each exercise varying amounts of control over the thinking and living in our culture. Christian supernaturalism, which preached the existence of God and the importance of spiritual faith, found itself in competition with modernism's naturalism, which gave high value to human reason and empirical science in a universe without God.

Postmodern thought is not just what came next in the human attempt to know all things. Rather, it is the end result of failures latent within modern thought without God. Modernism (or modern atheism) fails to stand on its own assumptions, since without God there seems to be no purpose or meaning to human existence, achievement, or struggle. Where modernism has failed as a worldview, postmodernism has stepped in to try to shore up the foundation.

Postmodernism is not so much a replacement for a modernism gone awry as it is an attempt to avoid the consequences of a world without God. No God means no human personhood, no absolutes in morality, no purpose, no meaning, and no future. There is a growing relativism without God (truth is related to the individual), so what is true for you in morals may not be true for me. With postmodern thought the full implications of relativism are present. In fact, in postmodernism there is a lack of confidence in humanity ever knowing truth or values. We are on our own; hence postmodernism offers a very negative outlook.

I HAVE A QUESTION

I keep reading the term relativism or something like it. What does that mean exactly? I am learning that I have to pay attention to any words ending in "ism."

Usually "ism" words mean that I am saying something about a philosophical point of view that a lot of people have talked about. Relativism means "related to." In our subject here, relativism in truth means that truth is related only to me. I determine what is true for me. Or in the case of ethics, relativism means that ethical decisions are related only to me; there are no absolutes in morality related to the God of the universe. I decide for myself what is right or wrong for me. Obviously, relativistic thought is rejecting the idea of one, absolute truth above all others or that there may be absolutes in ethics that apply to all of us.

It is interesting that ethical relativists have to make an absolute statement in order to deny that absolutes exist. Obviously there is something wrong with the truth claim for relativism.

Modern thought represents dependence on reason and empiricism. Postmodern thought emerges when people despair of ever knowing any ultimate truth. Once the hope in universal truth is lost, as it seems to be in our increasingly secular culture, then personal knowledge and experience become the favored tools to understand reality. Knowledge in postmodern thought, therefore, has been moved from the objective reality of the scientist to the private world of human experience.

The postmodern view of the person is not the Christian view of the human being as the image of God. The postmodern person is found in individual choice and experience. Underneath this change in the view of self is a shift in the view of how one knows anything, a shift from more objective knowledge to more subjective experience. Postmodern thought does not deny the physical realm, but it says that empiricism and science give a limited perspective of a complex reality. In this sense, postmodernism makes a good point. Modern science needs the critique that observers, even science observers, color their perceptions. But to move from that critique to denying any absolutes or fixed points in knowledge is extreme.

The shift to postmodern thought has been accompanied by a belief in moral relativism. Relativistic postmodern thought is seen in the worldview of secular humanism, where a secular (not sacred) world has produced human personhood with feelings of purpose and value and, thus, the human person, rather than God, becomes the center of all values. Another postmodern thought pattern is found in the worldview of atheistic existentialism, where there is no trust in human knowledge and potential, and so all life becomes absurd. Human life is absurd because human personal desires always exceed the naturalistic world's abilities to meet those desires. Modernism was optimistic. Postmodernism exhibits despair. Modernism looked to replace Christian morals with scientific absolutes. Postmodernism says, "It's all relative."

In the next chapter we will discuss the worldview known as naturalism, or it could be called atheistic naturalism. The postmodern reactions to the worldview of naturalism and its problems are the worldviews of secular humanism, atheistic existentialism, pantheism, and the New Age movement. All of these postmodern viewpoints try to do something different in their explanations about human nature in order to pass all the tests of a worldview.

While Christian theism is a premodern worldview, it can also be considered a postmodern viewpoint. During the late 1950s and 1960s, there was a resurgence of interest in all things going beyond the "mere-matter" views of naturalism, including all religious viewpoints. But Christian theism was also the original viewpoint in Europe that declined into or was rejected by the rise of modernism and naturalism. Therefore, I am seeing Christian theism almost as bookends around this conversation about current worldviews. I could begin by describing Christian theism in the next section, but I choose to end the book with the Christian worldview because I am illustrating how well Christian theism fits the tests of a worldview to which we are subjecting all these worldviews. I believe in Christian theism and the personal relationship with Jesus Christ, not just by assumption with absolutely no evidence to support it, but because my reason says that Christian theism is the optimal choice for a world and life view.

Filling out a matrix comparing modernism and postmodernism is not easy because there are many different postmodern systems of thought, including elements of historic Christianity. In the chart I have placed general beliefs in the postmodern cells that fit at least some of the postmodern systems of thought.

BELIEFS	MODERNISM	POSTMODERNISM
REALITY	Physical universe	Physical universe
KNOWLEDGE	Sensory knowledge	Experiential knowledge
HUMAN NATURE	Mere biology, animal	Personal human beings
HUMAN PROBLEMS	Genetics, brain	Blocked self-potential

BELIEFS	MODERNISM	POSTMODERNISM
SOLUTIONS TO HUMAN PROBLEMS	Pills, surgery, genetic engineering	Self-image building
HUMAN VALUE	No higher value	Different value than animal
HUMAN PURPOSE	Survival of the human race	Self-fulfillment
ETHICS	Whatever promotes survival	Whatever you feel like
SUFFERING	Little value to suffering	Avoid suffering if possible
MEANING IN LIFE	None	What meaning you make of it
HUMAN DESIRE	Just desires for food and sex	Genuine desires in addition to the physical

I HAVE A QUESTION

How can you teach on different worldviews when you don't even believe in them? It is easy to set up the frameworks of different worldviews and then, with your biases in place, just knock them down.

Good point, and good question. And the answer has to apply to everything we study. We all start with assumptions, and we have to be careful that those assumptions do not turn into biases or dogmatic beliefs with which we construe the world of facts only in our way. Yes, I am beginning with Christian assumptions, but I am willing to subject each worldview to the same three standard tests of truth and worldviews. I am not separating the world of faith from the world of learning. Beliefs and presuppositions will definitely influence me, but the educated person is careful to test beliefs and avoid losing out on the truth. The only other option is to believe in what is called skepticism, which says that no one can truly know truth apart from one's controlling biases.

I prefer instead to look at different, current options on truth in the world around me and use some standard ways of thinking to evaluate them. And I certainly believe that my Christian worldview should be subjected to the same rational scrutiny. Your objection works both ways in that I suspect Christianity has been rejected by many people who are only using their biases and knocking down the Christian straw man, instead of seeing the rational side of the Christian faith and life view.

SOME TERMS TO THINK ABOUT

modernism. Think of the modern age of science and reason. Think of Mr. Spock of Star Trek. Think of atheism. Think occasionally of science versus the Bible.

postmodernism. Think of a more recent time period, when people relax a bit on believing in spiritual things. They are into feelings as a source of knowledge and not just scientific discoveries. Think about poetry; do not think about instructions to assemble a bicycle.

moral relativism. Think of this—"It's my body, and I decide what's right for me to do with it. Religious choice is a private, personal thing. It is up to me to decide what is right and wrong for me. You can decide for yourself, and I will decide for myself."

SEVEN

Naturalism
Biological Machines

One of the greatest tragedies of our age is that so many Christians allowed themselves, particularly in the last century, to be frightened away from proclaiming the full message of biblical Christianity by the notion that it was scientifically out of date or discredited.

DONALD M. MACKAY

IF THE WORLDVIEW OF naturalism were pictured by a puzzle box top, what would the picture be? I imagine a beautiful picture of an ocean teaming with fish and a mountain covered with pine trees. In the center I see chimpanzees fussing around each other, and some machinelike-faced human beings nearby doing the same with their lawns and automobiles. The sky is filled with clouds and birds. However, the very top of the picture, beyond the sky, is dark and empty. There is nothing up there. There is nature in the picture but no supernature. There are living plants and animals, but there is no personhood in those beings and no God or heaven above.

Naturalism as a worldview gets its name from its belief that all reality is natural and not supernatural. Naturalism in this context is a nice word for atheism. René Descartes (1596–1650), a theist, set the stage for the coming of naturalism as a worldview with his dualism. Cartesian dualism split the world into those things that are

---

Epigraph. Donald M. Mackay, *The Clock Work Image* (Downers Grove, Ill.: InterVarsity, 1974), 105.

immaterial and those things that are material, thus permitting the study of material reality without recourse to spiritual explanations. Christian theists should not reject all of naturalism because of its atheism. Christians also believe in the natural order; however, they reject the idea that only matter exists in the universe.

Naturalism says all reality is matter/energy of some sort—matter and energy being two different forms of the same thing. The word for this is *materialism*—all is matter. There are no gods, ghosts, demons, spirits, or souls. Another belief of naturalism in the same line of thought is *determinism*. This means that every effect in the universe of matter and behavior has a prior physical cause. The universe is a closed system, and there is no input from God or free minds.

Knowledge to a naturalist arises from sensory experience. If all is matter, then my senses will have access to everything. Sensory knowledge is known as empiricism or sensory empiricism, which means knowledge comes through the senses. I learn from what I can see, hear, taste, touch, and smell, and however my scientific instruments can expand on those senses. The real problem with the naturalistic form of knowing is not empiricism. I believe in empiricism, that I can learn through my senses. But I also believe that there is more out there in the spiritual realm than my senses can perceive. Naturalism comes with a self-imposed ignorance when it pronounces that there is nothing out there but matter. When it does so, it is opting for a radical empiricism, which means I can learn *only* through my senses. Since this is a starting assumption of naturalism, this is clearly prejudging the case for spiritual life in human beings or for the existence of God. Such thinking leaves the naturalist open to accusations of circular reasoning.

I HAVE A QUESTION

What is circular reasoning?

Circular reasoning means arguing in a circle. Sometimes it is called "begging the question," but why don't you just remember the words "arguing in a circle," for they will give you a hint of the meaning. Circular reasoning means using an assumption to support ideas or findings that end up showing that original assumption. For example, a naturalist could say, "All is matter. Therefore, I feel free to use just empiricism or my senses to discover truth about human nature. Why use ways of knowing in addition to physics, chemistry, and biology when there is nothing out there but matter? And guess what, wherever I look, I have found only matter and human bodies and brains—no God, no souls, just matter. In other words, Christian teaching is wrong."

What is the value of an argument like this? The naturalist already believed there was no God or souls, and that naturalistic belief allowed him to search only with matter-detecting tools. Is it any wonder that the atheist finds no God or human immaterial souls? This circular reasoning reminds me of the atheistic Russian cosmonauts years ago, who looked out the window of their space capsule and said triumphantly, "We don't see a God anywhere out here."

The next beliefs in the naturalistic worldview concern human nature, and they flow from what has been covered in the beliefs about reality and knowledge. In naturalism the human being is seen as a biological machine. That belief does not come from evidences in biological and psychological research but is an end result of logical thought. "If the entire universe is mere matter and I am a part of the universe, then I too am mere matter. All the matter in the universe is determined; therefore, I am determined."

It is not so much research in scientific laboratories that demonstrates that human beings are biological machines, but it is the guiding assumptions of naturalism that have prejudged the case on human nature. The rest of the beliefs in naturalism then fall into place: human beings have no value, purpose, or meaning except in the relativism of choosing what we want to be true. There is no God to proclaim His absolutes.

In the naturalistic worldview, human problems must come from errant biology or genetics. I am just a gene's way of making another gene. The solutions to crime and depression will be found in neuro-chemistry, not religion. Purpose becomes survival in the evolutionary scheme of things, and ethical choices become whatever ensures reproductive success and the survival of one's own genes.

Christians should hold to a limited form of naturalism and at the same time believe that God exists. There is nothing wrong with naturalism per se. However, an atheistic naturalism (no God) runs into severe intellectual difficulties. There is a material world out there, and it does run by laws of cause and effect. In fact, the Christian worldview will be a form of super-"naturalism"—the natural is real and important, but there is a world and God beyond the natural. This supernaturalistic belief also says that God has communicated with and entered the world of the natural.

The Naturalistic Worldview: Machine Persons

BELIEFS	NATURALISM
REALITY	**Naturalism:** The universe is a natural place, and there are no supernatural beings. The universe is all there is, and it is a closed system. **Materialism:** All is matter/energy. **Determinism:** Matter is determined—for every effect there is a prior, physical cause.
KNOWLEDGE	**Sensory empiricism:** Knowledge comes from sensory experience, from your senses. **Radical empiricism:** An extreme form of empiricism that says there is no need for any other method of knowing beyond empiricism. **Logical positivism:** A philosophical system that embraces radical empiricism.

BELIEFS	NATURALISM
HUMAN NATURE	**Biological machine:** Human beings are just so much biological material, and like all matter they are determined. There are no minds or souls, only brains. **Reductionism:** This is a philosophy that explains the complex or mental in human beings by reference only to mere biology or mere animal. Reductionism says, "Human beings are nothing but functioning brains or are nothing but higher animals."
HUMAN PROBLEMS	**Physical causes—genetics, psychological conditioning, brain chemistry:** Problems ranging from mental illness, crime, anger, and war are the products of something wrong in the natural realm of the person. Sin nature or sin is an outmoded concept in the worldview of the naturalist.
SOLUTIONS TO HUMAN PROBLEMS	**Behavior modification, genetic engineering, personality-altering drugs:** These treat the physical nature of the person and assume that is all there is.
HUMAN VALUE	**Arbitrary value in the human race:** Your genes (the human race) will survive, even if you do not.
HUMAN PURPOSE	**Reproductive success (survival of the fittest):** A human being is a gene's way to make another gene.
ETHICS	**Whatever promotes survival of the human race is good and moral:** If the behavior helps us survive, then it is moral behavior. **Is = ought ethics:** Whatever human behavior has survived down through the ages and has not destroyed the cultures embracing it must be okay and moral.
SUFFERING	**No purpose to suffering:** We shoot injured horses. We talk about euthanasia for the terminally ill, the hopelessly insane, and for the elderly. Why let them suffer?
MEANING IN LIFE	**Individual human lives and world history run in cycles:** There is no overall story or meaning to daily events.

BELIEFS	NATURALISM
HUMAN DESIRE	**Deep human desires for truth, justice, romance, and God are really distorted physical drives for food, sex, or safety:** Your inner desires are Freudian (psychological) or sociobiological (genetic) in origin.

I HAVE A QUESTION

I didn't follow the short definition of the words logical positivism and reductionism. What do they mean?

Those can be tough concepts, so let me expand a bit. Logical positivism is sometimes called positivism. It is a branch of philosophy that embraces radical empiricism, which says that if you cannot get an empirical answer to a question, then it is a meaningless question to ask. It is okay to ask if there is gold in Colorado, because we can see the gold. But to the logical positivist, it is meaningless to ask if divorce is wrong. We cannot get an empirical answer to that question, so let us not ask it. Obviously naturalistic, logical positivism as a philosophy has a lot less to say about the larger questions in life that are of interest to us.

Now let me explain the word *reductionism*. Can you see the word *reduce* here? Reductionism is the naturalistic philosophy that says you can reduce the complicated in human beings to mere biology or animal behavior. There is no real love, just animal sexual responses. Religion is just superstitious behavior. This has been humorously called the philosophy of nothing buttery, that is, "Man is nothing but an animal."

Let me further define one of the important ideas we have just seen in the naturalistic worldview.

Is = Ought

This equation is the naturalistic answer to the question about how to define what is morally right and wrong. Survival is the key in naturalism as to what is good. If some behavior helps you or your race to survive, then let us call that behavior morally good. If some behavior hurts your survival, then let us call it morally bad. Love is good because it helps us survive. Atomic bombs are bad because they kill us in large numbers. Actually, some have suggested that atomic bombs are good because thoughts about their horrific outcome deter the outbreak of some conflicts. The difficulty with this prediction ethic is how anyone can predict the survival of the human race based upon certain behaviors. Can we accurately predict your survival or the human race's survival based upon your cheating on your taxes or your adultery?

Therefore, naturalists, who cannot accurately predict the future, look to the past to see what has survived for thousands of years in human behavior. Those behaviors that have survived up until now must be good. Homosexuality has not wiped us out as a culture, therefore, it must be morally okay. Adultery has not destroyed us, so it must be okay. This is the "is = ought" ethic; anything that *is* (that has survived until today) *ought* to be (is morally okay). One serious problem with the "is = ought" ethic is that it allows for any behavior, no matter how obnoxious or heinous, that has survived down through time to be called moral and good. Adultery may be declared okay with this ethic, but so will child abuse and rape. The naturalistic worldview is not going to pass the third test of a worldview since we cannot even conceive of a world in which it is moral to abuse children and rape women. Naturalism thus fails to provide an adequate basis for making moral decisions.

I HAVE A QUESTION

It seems like scientists and atheists come up with ethical guidelines just like anyone else. Where do they get them?

People who hold the naturalistic worldview are not necessarily evil and immoral people. They have moral guidelines that may be as good as any Christian morality. However, they are not getting their guidelines from the naturalistic worldview, which, as we have seen with the "is = ought" problem, actually approves horrible, existentially repugnant behaviors that have survived over time. These naturalists "smuggle" their ethical guidelines into their system from some other worldview, usually Christian theism. Then the question becomes, if your worldview does not provide you with the basis for living your life, why do you believe it? If we cannot conceive of living without ethical guidelines of some sort, then let us look for a worldview that has a basis for them. The only other choice is to avow that there are no absolutes in ethics and let our lives and civilization decay into anarchy.

Remember that when you say "scientists" that very few scientists are atheists. Many, in fact, are strong Christians. Radical empiricism, not science, is the problem in the naturalistic worldview.

Testing Naturalism

In terms of our three tests of a worldview, naturalism fails the test of evidence, passes the test of logical consistency, and fails the test of existential repugnance.

The Test of Evidence

As much boasting as there is to the contrary, the naturalistic worldview does not describe human beings in a way that lines up with the evidence. To say that human beings are mere biological machines, or just higher animals, ignores much evidence to the contrary. This is not an argument against evolution but a stating of the clear differences between human beings and the animal world. And the differences seem to be there, not to guarantee reproductive success, but to contribute to human personhood. Humans are self-aware and possess symbolic, meaningful, and ethical existence. The evidence is seen in our self-reports on our own experience, the worldwide nature of religious experience, the drama of human history, and the nature of the human brain (the complexity of which seems far more designed for personhood than survival). Human beings seem more designed to read Shakespeare than to locate bananas and grass.

These human differences will lead us into the argument for supernaturalism called the apologetic from desire, which is covered in more detail in a later chapter. This argument essentially says that human beings are overbuilt for the world. Why would there be a creature whose brain allows him to be spread out in time and symbol and exist in metaphorical, meaningful, and ethical frames of reality in a flat universe of mere matter? The least impressionable feature of our mental existence is our sensory input system. But naturalistic thinkers of the last century insisted on a stimulus-response definition of the person, just like the current age of naturalism points to the marvels of DNA and brain chemistry to explain the nature of the person. All that nature needed was an efficient banana detector, but what it got was Mozart, Einstein, Mother Theresa, Stephen Spielberg, and the rest of us marvelous human beings. I could present much more evidence, but suffice it to say that atheists themselves, secular humanists and atheistic existentialists, and religious thinkers (of whom many are excellent scientists) see the evidence for human nature and would rather explain personhood than explain personhood away.

The Test of Logical Consistency

The naturalistic worldview to its credit is logically consistent. We can most easily see the logical consistency in the worldviews we are studying by looking at their beliefs about reality and about human nature. If all of the universe is matter, and human beings are a part of the universe, then human beings are mere matter according to the naturalistic worldview. That is logical. If all matter is determined by laws of cause and effect, and human beings are mere matter, then human beings, no matter what their feelings to the contrary, are determined and not free. In the case of the naturalistic worldview, it appears that presupposition, not empirical data, is speaking more loudly on what human nature is. But is it not better to be logical than illogical? I think so, and I credit the naturalistic thinker with that consistency. However, other worldviews, such as secular humanism, have sought to change atheistic naturalism in order to keep a personal and unique view of human nature.

The Test of Existential Repugnance

The naturalistic worldview fails the third test of a worldview, the test of existential repugnance. This test asks, Can you live as if this belief is true? Can you imagine human beings living as if humans are mere biological machines? Can a naturalist live as if he is only a machine with no free will (reductionism)? No one lives as if crimes come from determined individuals who, therefore, should go unpunished. We do live as if strong influence is possible, but not determinism. No one lives as if people were no more valuable than roadkill. If you cannot live out the naturalistic worldview, then why believe it is true? This third test of a worldview does not prove that naturalism is incorrect, but it does caution against being hasty in accepting a worldview that runs against the very nature of the mental life of human beings, the dominant creatures on the planet.

The Consequences of a Failing Naturalistic Worldview

Over the last three hundred years, there has been an erosion of the Christian worldview and the Christian concept of the person and life. Christian theism's view of a universe created and actively ruled by God has gradually lost ground, first to the worldview of deism and then to atheistic naturalism. According to deism God did create the world, but He has absented himself from it. The step from theism to an atheistic naturalism was not hard to make over the bridge created by deism. The *Zeitgeist* (spirit of the age) has changed from believing that God exists and is the creator of the natural order to believing there is no God and only the natural order exists. This shift of worldview seems to have given birth to two crises of thinking and living: anthropological and epistemological.

The Anthropological Crisis

The anthropological crisis is the "man," or human nature, crisis. Simply stated, if there is no God, if the natural order is all there is or ever was, then human nature is just a part of the natural order. There is no meaning, significance, or purpose to human existence. Free will is an illusion or a cruel joke of evolution since all matter, including human matter, is ruled by deterministic laws of cause and effect. Thus, there is no way to determine right from wrong, and discussions about absolute values are irrelevant. There is no meaning or purpose to the suffering all human beings must endure. In such a world, human life seems absurd to the atheistic existentialist.

The anthropological crisis does not exist for animals because only human beings seem to clearly feel the opposite of what the atheistic, naturalistic worldview believes. We long for truth, heroism, justice, beauty, morality, and eternity. In other words, we long for more than bananas and grass. We experience a good measure of the feelings of freedom, strive to discover self-worth, correct our immoral behavior, and seek to piece the behaviors and pains of daily life into some larger picture of meaning in the universe. Our very being cries out against this naturalistic worldview that ignores the inner world of self.

The Epistemological Crisis

Epistemology refers to how we know; so the epistemological crisis is a crisis in knowledge. Naturalism has resulted in a loss of confidence in the human ability to know truth. How did naturalism produce such a crisis in knowing when it was supreme confidence in human reason that helped kick off the advances in naturalistic thinking in the first place? It seems ironic that confidence in human reason during the humanistic Renaissance and the later Enlightenment has resulted in a loss of confidence in human reason.

In the naturalistic worldview, human beings are just a piece of nature and, therefore, just determined machines. What we desire and claim as truth is not the product of an unbiased search for truth but the result of our psychological and chemical histories. If we are determined, then truth is undiscoverable because we can never know that it was not our environment or brain chemistry leading us to believe in certain things. This is especially true of moral truth, and so relativism—what is true for the individual—replaces the search for absolute truth.

And this is the end-result type of person we find today in our naturalistic culture, one who is not concerned with absolute truth but who looks to his own desires and experiences as guides to behavior. That is the picture of relativism. The current naturalistic doctrine is: either absolute truth does not exist, or it is undiscoverable. What has been lost is the idea of one universal truth into which all other discoveries and truths must fit. This Christian concept of one overarching truth gives rise to the name *university,* which means "one truth." Christian "universities," therefore, should be places where we resist the anthropological and epistemological crises of our day as we go about our business of learning the truth.

SOME TERMS TO THINK ABOUT

anthropological crisis. If naturalism is true, then we are not persons with real meaning, purpose, and significance to our lives. We are just accidental products of blind evolution, present on the earth for a brief number of years; just blips on the universe's screen of billions of years of existence.

determinism. The absence of free choice. It seems reasonable to say that there are many times in our lives when we may not be free in our decisions. But the determinism spoken of here says that human beings are never able to exercise free choice.

epistemological crisis. If all matter is determined, then the very words that come out of my mouth, the very thoughts in my head, are also determined by physical forces beginning billions of years ago with the big bang. There is no freedom to love or to choose virtue. There is no discovery of truth, because, for all I know, I am simply sprouting what my genetic roots programmed me for.

materialism. Human beings are entirely described by matter. The human mind, therefore, is merely a by-product of brain activity.

reductionism. This is a philosophy that reduces the complex things about human nature to the simple animal or biological level. There is no political behavior but only primate struggles over territory. There is no true search for God but only meaning-searching, neural networks in the parietal lobe of the brain.

zeitgeist. *Zeit* is German for time, and *geist* means ghost or spirit. *Zeitgeist* therefore means spirit of the times. It is another word for worldview—the mental spirit of what people believe and under which they operate.

EIGHT

Secular Humanism

A "Street" Version of Naturalism

When the Bible says that man is created in the image of a personal
God, it gives us a starting-point. No humanistic system has pro-
vided a justification for man to begin with himself.

FRANCIS A. SCHAEFFER

SECULAR HUMANISM IS A cousin of atheistic naturalism. It is the same atheism with one glaring exception. Secular humanism will not deny humanity's humanness no matter how empty the cosmos is of any personal starting point. For this livable version of naturalism, let us imagine that we were just handed a giant puzzle representing the worldview of secular humanism. We look at the box top to see what kind of world this worldview is claiming. We see in this picture a human population alive with personality, rich in thought and emotions, and busy with very personal activities. However, all this glowing humanness is placed under a completely dark sky. There is no God in His heaven watching over things in this worldview.

Epigraph. Francis A. Schaeffer, *Escape from Reason* (Downers Grove, Ill.: InterVarsity, 1968), 87.

A Summary of Secular Humanism

Secular humanism is a "street" version of atheistic natural-ism; that is, it is an atheism that ordinary people are living in the streets. This belief is rarely a firm, thinking atheism but is more of an "I-don't-know-and-I-don't-care" agnosticism. Either way, athe-ism or agnosticism, God is left out and ignored. Secular human-ism detaches itself from the logic of the naturalistic worldview that leaves human beings as biological machines. As a worldview, secu-lar humanism allows its adherents to believe that they are persons with purpose and at the same time to remain atheists or ironclad agnostics. Secular humanism says that the universe is only matter (secular), but I am more than mere matter (humanism). Secular hu-manism will, therefore, pass the test of evidence by admitting to the evidence for human personhood and feelings of value. However, it will fail the test of logical consistency because it says, "All reality is just matter and I am a part of reality, but somehow I am more than mere matter."

To understand secular humanism, one needs to understand the failures of modern naturalism. Naturalism as a worldview holds to a materialistic, deterministic universe, in which human nature is logically reduced to mere biological machinery. This view may be logically consistent, but it denies our experience of humanness and leaves us with no basis for meaning or purpose to life. Secular humanism's "rebellion" from naturalism claims that inner experi-ence, not logic and science, is the primary basis for knowing. In the spirit of this way of knowing about the important directions in life, the 1960s rang with the cry, "If it feels good, do it."

Very few atheists or agnostics attempt to live according to the naturalistic worldview in which human beings are seen as biologi-cal machines. In such a view there is no meaning or purpose to ex-istence, and there are no absolute standards to guide behavior. Most people who have a naturalistic view of life live out their naturalism by asserting that the universe is a materialistic, deterministic place but that human beings are the great exception. Human beings, unlike the universe that spawned them, have personhood, which includes free will, self-awareness, and symbolic existence. Human beings also have value and meaning to their lives. The secular humanist says that the universe is not sacred but is secular—without any God. Even so, claims the secular humanist, human beings are more than mere matter and more than determining genes and conditioned reflexes. They are human and not just animal. Thus, the name of this amended version of naturalism is secular humanism.

For Christians the problem with secular humanism should not be in the word *humanism* but in the word *secular*. *Secular* means that the basis for everything we see and experience in the universe is atheistic; there is no God. In other words, the universe is secular, not sacred. *Humanism,* on the other hand, is a perfectly acceptable word for Christians and their worldview. Christian theism sees the person of God as the source for personhood and value in human beings, who were created in His image. Christians believe that human beings are filled with potential, although that potential is limited by their fallen, sinful condition. "Christian humanism" makes logical sense since human personhood has its source in the personhood of God. "Secular humanism," on the other hand, is a logical inconsistency.

A belief in "Christian" humanism means that things human should be very important and not distasteful to Christians. This is another argument for the Christian interest in the liberal arts. Some Christians view human productions in the arts and sciences as worthless, humanistic endeavors as opposed to other more spiritual and less worldly activities. This is certainly not the view of the Christian liberal-arts college. Christian students should guard their hearts and minds as they watch films, read novels, listen to music, explore scientific knowledge, and enter the professions. But it would hardly be Christian to look down on such activities as less spiritual or a waste of time.

I HAVE A QUESTION

My pastor says all the time that secular humanism is the enemy of Christians. Is he right?

Your pastor is right concerning secular humanism, which is similar to atheism. Secular humanists have a high view of human nature and our purpose and value, but they do so from their foundation of atheism, which is secular and not sacred. The problem is that matter alone cannot provide the source for human value and meaning. Christian humanism, by the way, makes perfect sense. We believe in the value of human beings from the standpoint of a creator God who created them, values them, and died for them. The problem that often arises with rejecting secular humanism is that we also reject human things like movies or dancing, simply because they are not "sacred." God created the world and human beings, and it is very much a part of Christian theology to be involved in enjoying, studying, and redeeming this world for God.

The Worldview of Secular Humanism: Fake Persons

BELIEFS	SECULAR HUMANISM
REALITY	**Naturalism:** All is natural, not supernatural. **Materialism:** All is matter/energy. There is no God or spirit or soul in the universe. **Determinism:** All matter is determined by laws of cause and effect.
KNOWLEDGE	**Human experience:** This method of knowing involves inner feelings and inclinations as opposed to thinking and reasoning. Human reason built atomic bombs. Human feelings desire peace. **Sensory experience:** Empirical knowledge (through your senses) is acceptable for knowledge in the material realm but is not the primary method of learning about things human.

BELIEFS	SECULAR HUMANISM
HUMAN NATURE	**More than matter:** Human beings are persons with freedom and self-consciousness. **We are good:** Human beings are not fallen beings, as the church says, but are inwardly directed toward those behaviors that are moral and good. Your deepest feelings will tell you what is good.
HUMAN PROBLEMS	**Personal potential is blocked:** We are capable of goodness and happiness, but much of that potential is blocked by rules and regulations, often by religious or parental rules.
SOLUTIONS TO HUMAN PROBLEMS	**Unblock personal potential:** Free up human beings to be all that they can be. Feelings have guided us successfully through millions of years of evolution. Why not trust basic human feelings and emotions all the time? **Religion is not usually helpful:** Religions seem unusually negative and limiting with regard to personhood. Religions restrict human behavior and label human beings "sinful."
HUMAN VALUE	**High value:** This is an arbitrary decision to say we are of high value. If a group of squirrels were reading this book, they would be saying that squirrels are of high value.
HUMAN PURPOSE	**To discover self and self-potential:** To rise above your material existence and become fully human. To make decisions for yourself. To find love and meaningful work.
ETHICS	**Individual feelings:** If it feels right for you, then it is right. Who knows more about you and your needs than you do? **Is = ought is the basis for ethics:** In determining what is ethically correct, it is too difficult to predict the future of our actions, but we can look at the past and see what behaviors have survived. If homosexual behavior has survived for 5,000 years, then it must be okay. If murder has survived for 5,000 years, then it must be okay too.

BELIEFS	SECULAR HUMANISM
	Relativism: Ethical decisions are related to you, not to your church, or your nation, or your peer group. You decide what is right and wrong relative to you and your needs.
SUFFERING	**There is no meaning to suffering:** You may grow from hard times, but suffering or martyrdom is rarely a good choice of behavior.
MEANING IN LIFE	**Meaning to individual experience and choice:** Meaning in life comes when self is expanded into all of its potential. That is why secular humanism has sometimes been called the human potential movement.
HUMAN DESIRE	**Trust your deep desires:** Your innermost feelings and desires will lead in the right directions for your survival and happiness. What if someone desires to kill children? The answer is that he could not really feel that way, so we should help him get in touch with his true innermost desires.

Testing Secular Humanism

How does secular humanism fair on the three tests of a world-view? It passes the test of evidence, fails the test of logical consistency, and passes the test of existential repugnance.

The Test of Evidence

Secular humanism passes the test of evidence because it admits to the personhood of human beings. There is much evidence to support our personhood in the subjective worlds of human experience, the arts, and the religions of the world. The secular humanist relies heavily upon the personal feelings of human beings for this belief. However, secular humanism does tend to ignore things like sins and the sin nature. In general, secular humanism does not concentrate on the animal in man. Secular humanism passes this first test of evidence at the expense of failing the second test.

The Test of Logical Consistency

Do all assumptions in secular humanism's worldview agree with each other? Logic would say, "All the universe is matter. I am a part of the universe. Therefore, I am just matter." Mere matter has only arbitrary value or purpose. "I am matter, a child of nature," says the secular humanist, "but I have high value and purpose beyond the world of matter." The secular humanist will say that being illogical does not matter. A heavy dependence on rationality, reason, and empiricism has led to wars and the failure to see what human beings can be. The secular, humanistic stance is: It is better to be illogical than to miss the essential data of human life altogether. That is an excellent point. However, I would hate to have a worldview that fits the facts on human nature but requires me to be illogical in order to believe in it. We want a worldview that can hold on to human nature and at the same time remain rational.

I HAVE A QUESTION

Does everything have to be so logical in worldviews or Christianity?

No. Christianity is not always logical and rational. In fact, most people probably would think of Christianity or faith in other religions as anything but rational. Christianity is more often accused of being just faith, flimsy emotions, and otherworldly concerns. I hope your question means you are beginning to see the very important and rational side to Christianity. On the other hand, there is much to the Christian faith that requires belief beyond what the evidences can reach. Emotions and feelings also play a vital part in the experience of the Christian life. Your worldview as an interplay between reason and faith is what this book is all about.

The Test of Existential Repugnance

I gave secular humanism a "thumbs up" on this test, the test of living out the worldview. But my appraisal comes with some hesitation. It must be said that secular humanism is usually very livable. It is good to be able to say that I am a person with value, meaning, and purpose. What is better, however, is to have worldview assumptions that can support such a high view of human nature. The secular humanist has to live illogically, when he says that he is more than the universe that spawned him. Secular humanism always leaves one with the uncomfortable notion that something is incomplete in that worldview's explanation for humanity. In the next chapter, we will look at atheistic existentialism as a worldview that claims to be able to deny God, uplift human nature, and remain logical all the while.

I HAVE A QUESTION

What did you mean by "is = ought"?

Is = ought" means any behavior that is, that exists, ought to be considered moral and acceptable human behavior. This is the ethic of many atheists because they assume (without God) there are no absolutes in ethical matters. They are letting survival (an ever-present evolutionary guide) be the standard for right and wrong. If some behavior does not kill us or our culture, it must be okay. Good or "moral" behaviors must benefit us and not destroy our chances of surviving.

SOME TERMS TO THINK ABOUT

humanism. Pertaining to human beings. It usually stands for the good and potential in human individuals and society.

is = ought. Anything that is, or exists in reasonable numbers down through time, ought to be considered morally okay. Do you think you could recognize if someone you knew employed this ethic in his choices? How about the teenager who tells her mom, "But everybody my age is doing it!"?

secular. The opposite of sacred. Think of this as defining something for which there is no religious connection. Many times it is just a nice word for atheism.

NINE

Atheistic Existentialism

"Freak" Persons

Mother died today. Or, maybe, yesterday; I can't be sure.

ALBERT CAMUS

But two months dead, nay, not so much, not two! So excellent a
king . . . so loving to my mother.

SHAKESPEARE

THE PUZZLE BOXES ARE beginning to pile up around us now. Every one of them is a proposed view of the picture that the same set of puzzle pieces inside the boxes make. In these chapters we are looking at these box-top worldview pictures that claim to be satisfactory guides for our lives. This worldview search is not just an academic exercise for the philosophically minded, for our lives and decisions are dependent upon how we see reality. Now we have been handed the box top of the puzzle of atheistic existentialism. What picture does it show? The sky is still dark, there is no God in the universe, and human life seems more depressed and bored than the secular humanist's picture of reality.

Epigraph. Albert Camus, *The Stranger* (New York: Vintage Books, 1942), 1; and Shakespeare, *Hamlet* (New York: Penguin, 1980), act 1, scene 2, lines 138–40.

A Summary of Atheistic Existentialism

The first thing to understand about atheistic existentialism is that it is a worldview trying to come to grips with the end results of atheistic naturalism. In the last 150 years, the worldview of naturalism has supposedly replaced Christian theism as the thinking person's worldview. Serious problems inherent in naturalism have led to two major alternatives to naturalism's view of human nature in an atheistic universe. These alternatives, which strongly affected American and European thought and life after World War II, are secular humanism and atheistic existentialism. First, let me briefly review the problems with atheistic naturalism and with the secular humanist's livable version of naturalism. Then I will examine the worldview of atheistic existentialism, which tries to offer a more intellectual alternative to these problems than does secular humanism.

Atheistic naturalism results in nihilism, a philosophy of despair and emptiness that paralyzes it as a livable worldview. Nihilism is a philosophy that denies the possibility of the discovery of truth and denies any purpose, meaning, or value to human lives. Nihilism is another word for the end results of believing in a world without God. If God does not exist, as the naturalist claims, then matter/energy is all there is and all that human life will ever be. The universe is a determined, closed system, and human beings are just complex machines. Thus, there is no basis for human beings to act significantly, to act morally, to act knowledgeably, to act purposefully, or to cling to hopes of their deep desires being met now or in the future.

Since such a despairing naturalism cannot be lived out by anyone, people by default often become secular humanists. A secular humanist ignores the logic of the natural universe giving rise to only natural creatures, and depends, instead, on the inner human feelings of personhood, value, and purpose. The secular humanist believes we have meaning, value, and purpose despite the absence of these in the natural universe, because our deepest feelings authenticate it. This is a "since-I-feel-it, it-must-be-so" mentality. To the secular humanist, human experience, not human experiment, becomes the dominant method of knowing.

Atheistic existentialism rejects the inconsistent thinking of secular humanism and gives a different way for humans to transcend the anthropological crisis of naturalism. Atheistic existentialism first of all remains atheistic. There is no God. But atheistic existentialists redefine human nature. Human beings have self-consciousness and self-determination by an evolutionary accident, and thus human beings can have some significance and value beyond unconscious matter. The atheistic existentialist believes that *existence precedes essence,* that is, that human beings exist and have evolved as conscious beings qualitatively distinct from plants and animals but they do not really become human beings in their essence until they start making conscious choices with their freedom. Choice, not a unique human brain, is what sets human nature apart from and above the world of nature. Thus each human person is free to choose his own nature and destiny, to create his own value and worth. Human life, however, is tragically absurd because our humanness with its deep desires stands alone and pitifully small against the backdrop of the immense, cold, impersonal machinery of a material universe. And death is the final absurdity when we, who have risen above the material universe, must inevitably sink back beneath its dark surface.

I HAVE A QUESTION

Slow down, please. I have no idea what you meant when you said that atheistic existentialists believe that existence precedes essence. Can you break it down for me?

Existence means biological existence—being born. When a baby is born, there is only a body, and there is not much there in terms of a self-conscious mind. Essence to Christians would mean something like soul, the essence of a being. But to the atheistic existentialist, there is in the baby nothing but physical existence, and what we call essence is really just the product of mental choices. The person is an existence but not really a special essence or soul that survives the death of the body. When choices begin in a human life, essence is present. When the choices stop at brain death, the essence is gone.

The Worldview of Atheistic Existentialism: Freak Persons

BELIEFS	ATHEISTIC EXISTENTIALISM
REALITY	**Naturalism:** This universe is a natural place, not a supernatural place. **Materialism:** Everything that exists in the universe is some form of matter or energy. There are no gods, ghosts, or demons. **Determinism:** Matter is locked into cause/effect relationships.
KNOWLEDGE	**Human experience:** Human feelings and desires. **Sensory experience:** What I can know with my senses.
HUMAN NATURE	**"Freak" personhood:** Human beings have the attributes of being persons: free will, self-consciousness, symbolic existence. But this inner life is accidental and does not matter.
HUMAN PROBLEMS	**Not coming to grips with one's absurd condition Biological, psychological, and cultural sources of human problems**
SOLUTIONS TO HUMAN PROBLEMS	**Admit to absurdity and make choices anyway:** Live as if your inner desires were of some value and had some impact on yourself and your world.
HUMAN VALUE	**No ultimate value**
HUMAN PURPOSE	**No ultimate purpose**

BELIEFS	ATHEISTIC EXISTENTIALISM
ETHICS	**No ultimate guide**
SUFFERING	**No purpose to suffering**
MEANING IN LIFE	**No meaning to life**
HUMAN DESIRE	**Absurd inner feelings that lead to nowhere:** Don't be led astray by these deep desires. For many it would be better to kill inner human desire rather than face the absurdity of their condition.

I HAVE A QUESTION

Will you please explain again what you mean by "freak" personality?

Freak personality to the atheistic existentialist means an accidental personality. Christians believe in persons with immortal souls created by God, who is a person. In the absence of a personal God, what atheistic existentialists see in human beings must be just the accidental product of evolution. You want to and can do so much more than you need to do in this material universe. You just need to find bananas, but you also have the mind to discover calculus, fall in love, and pen the most soul-wrenching poetry. You are a freak because that desire for calculus, romance, or justice does not mean you are in a higher world of such things. It just means you evolved beyond what was needed in order to survive physically. And those deep desires make the whole drama of life beyond bananas seem rather absurd. You are a freak, personal exception in a natural world.

The opposite Christian argument for all these high human abilities and deep desires is that humans were created for a world that contains those very things and more. I have said this before, but let me say it again. All nature needed was an efficient banana detector, but what it got was you. Either you are overbuilt for the world (freak), which is what the atheistic existentialist says, or the world is bigger than the natural realm, which is what Christians claim.

Testing Atheistic Existentialism

How does atheistic existentialism fair on the three tests of a worldview? It passes the tests of evidence and logical consistency, but fails the test of existential repugnance.

The Test of Evidence

The atheistic existential worldview passes the test of evidence because, like the secular humanist, it says that human beings are clearly beings above nature. Who can deny our symbolic existence, mental life, and moral search? But the atheistic existentialist now suffers the possibility of being inconsistent in believing in this grand nature of human beings in a strictly material universe.

The Test of Logical Consistency

The atheistic existentialist admits to the personal elements of human beings but calls us "freak" persons. That means that, yes, you are above the animal world, and you have self-consciousness, freedom, and symbolic existence, but those attributes are only the accidental products of evolution. Being a creature with language or self-awareness does not mean anything is special about you. You feel like an immortal being, but you are not. You long to find God, to rid yourself of guilt feelings, but none of that God stuff is true. So many of your problems come from these freakish changes, and you can feel the absurdity of life. You have a longing to love, where only sex exists. You possess real freedom of choice, but there is nothing to choose. Some atheistic existentialists would argue that it would be better for you if you had no such brain or that you had a prefrontal lobotomy to remove such humanness, and then you could go back to nibbling grass and peeling bananas with the rest of material nature.

The worldview of atheistic existentialism is internally consistent because it does not claim any value, meaning, or significance for human beings. This worldview claims only that humans have accidentally evolved deep feelings about their high value and central place within the universe. For the atheistic existentialist to believe in personhood is inconsistent with his or her atheism. However, to believe in "freak" or "accidental" personhood is consistent with an atheistic universe.

The Test of Existential Repugnance

This third test is failed by atheistic existentialism. No one can live as if these deep human feelings and values have no meaning. Atheistic existentialists come in two types. The more negative type says there is no meaning in life in spite of what your great mind longs for. Give it up. The more positive atheistic existentialist says live in the ways that fulfill these deep desires, even though, in the long run, it does not matter whether you live that way or not. The existential advice on one hand is to live with a shallow, flattened mind and emotions like Camus' lead character Meursault in *The Stranger*. He does not even seem to know or care when his mother died, today or yesterday! On the other hand is a more positive approach of some atheistic existentialists, who say we have to force ourselves to act in accordance with our inner desires even though we know such desire is all a sham. Such an approach says it is worthwhile to choose to love, pursue knowledge, and be constructive members of society, even though it does not matter in a world without God. This is why theistic existentialists claim that human life in an atheistic universe is absurd.

I HAVE A QUESTION

What do you mean that the atheistic existentialist believes that this life is absurd?

The atheistic existentialist thinks it is ridiculous to be living in a plain, ordinary, material world of bananas and grass and yet have a "higher" mind, which is an accidental product of evolution. It is ridiculous that we desire deep things like romance and eternity that are not out there in the material realm. Some atheistic existentialists say you would feel a lot better and less of this absurdity if you were just a mindless worm or a lobotomized human. Human beings fill their lives with novels and films as they feel the longing for romance, heroism, truth, justice, forgiveness, eternity, and purpose, none of which the material world can offer. It is absurd to be awake in a universe that is asleep.

Thus, to the atheistic existentialist, one's task in life is to create value and meaning where there is none. One does this by exercising human choice to create oneself. One problem with this is that there is no meaning to the words *good* or *value* when you define them as making a choice. Surely it is obvious that Hitler or yesterday's terrorist made choices that we would say were actions freely chosen and yet morally wrong. Atheistic existentialism offers an existence of meaning and purpose only because people choose to believe they exist with significance and value, even though their atheism says otherwise. We have free will for some unexplained reason, but, unfortunately, there is nothing to choose. Atheistic existentialism says to go ahead and choose anyway, and for that moment you may not be feeling the absurdity of life (i.e., deep desire in a shallow universe).

The truth is that making choices in the good directions of love, work, and meaning only serves to increase the absurdity of one's situation in an atheistic world. It does not really matter at all what you choose to do. Whether you are a sinner or a saint, what does it matter twenty-five million years from now in the great spiral drift of the galaxy, or twenty-five days from now in the traffic jams of Boston? Atheistic existentialism fails to produce a satisfactory explanation for the deep desires of the human heart. This failure opens our search for a satisfactory worldview to more spiritual options. Therefore, we now turn to pantheism and its more livable version, the New Age movement. And, finally, we will investigate Christian theism to see how it fares in explaining the deepest mysteries of human life.

SOME TERMS TO THINK ABOUT

absurdity. The human condition in a world without God: great thoughts but no one to share them with; deep love desires, but nothing but sex and reproductive efforts out there; moral feelings in an immoral world. What a deal, huh? All dressed up and nowhere to go.

Christian existentialism. No need to cover this here or in this book since this is a very different brand of existentialism as the name "Christian" might imply. See the writings of Søren Kierkegaard.

existence precedes essence. Human beings are essentially biological creatures, not souls in bodies, but with bodies that through choice "turn on" temporary souls.

TEN

Pantheism

Spirit Nonpersons

*But if God created the world, time is real. That's why Christianity,
like Judaism, takes history seriously. It is a historical religion, a story,
an eye-witness account of deeds and words in the world. Christianity
is "the gospel," the good* news. *But in Eastern religions, the only
gospel is that time is an illusion, that there is no news.*

PETER KREEFT

ONE GIANT PUZZLE WE HAVE just been given for this chapter's con-
sideration is the worldview of pantheism. The puzzle pieces inside
the boxes we are gathering in these chapters are all the same, no
matter what the box-top picture is. It is up to us to decide which
picture will give us the correct guide to assembling the puzzle. The
wrong box top on a giant puzzle would frustrate our puzzle-building
efforts. Similarly, having a wrong worldview will seriously endanger
our chances of putting a meaningful life together. The picture on
the pantheistic box top is more wild and colorful than the others.
The sky is a kaleidoscope of color and shape, and in the colors and
shapes below we notice human beings and other camouflaged forms
imbedded in the color splashes. There is a subtle pattern hidden in
the box-top picture no matter where in the picture we glance.

Dissatisfaction with atheistic explanations for reality and human

---

Epigraph. Peter Kreeft, *Between Heaven and Hell* (Downers Grove, Ill.: InterVarsity,
1982), 92–93.

nature has led to Western culture's increasing interest in pantheism. This pantheistic worldview sits cross-legged at the foundation of Eastern religions like Hinduism and Buddhism. Naturalism and atheistic existentialism claim no personal source for the personhood present in human nature. Therefore, the atheistic world is a cold, impersonal universe in which there can be no value, meaning, or purpose to human existence. In a deterministic, naturalistic scheme of things, human reason is not to be trusted, so many people today find the irrationalism of the Eastern worldviews attractive. After all, the science and rationality of the West in the company of relative ethics and a materialistic hedonism have not solved our personal and social problems. An atheistic foundation leads to the conclusion that human beings are all just biological machines without significance or purpose, yet people find it impossible to live as if there is no value or meaning in who they are and no purpose for living. Pantheism thus becomes an alternative mind-set to the searching minds in the West.

Instead of the atheist's cold, sterile view of the universe and man, some choose instead to build on the foundation of pantheism, which puts the word *spirit* back into our vocabulary when discussing the nature of the universe and human life. Whether that "spirit" is enough to explain the human personality and the depth of human thought and desire is debatable. In the 1960s American culture witnessed an increased interest in things spiritual, and particularly in Eastern religions and pantheism. The move to spiritual meditation and knowledge-seeking represented for some a welcome change from excessive rationalism and materialism, which left hollowed-out lives in their paths.

I HAVE A QUESTION

I want to know if it is okay for Christians to meditate. And how about yoga classes for exercise?

Yes, it is okay for Christians to meditate, and many Christians down through history have. It is even a good idea to encourage all Christians to develop some meditation in their times of prayer and Bible study. The difference between pantheistic meditation and the meditation in the Christian tradition is that Christian meditation is always meditation on something, whereas the Eastern mystic is emptying the mind. The Christian who meditates is trying to dismiss the hectic, random thoughts that fill a busy mind in order to concentrate more fully on something like the holiness of God or the love of God. The Eastern mystic wants to loose the contents of the senses and the mind in order to get rid of "self." The Christian meditates in order to worship God and lessen the self-centeredness he or she finds within. The Eastern mystic will meditate on a sound (a mantra such as "ommmm") or something irrational (such as the sound of one hand clapping) in order to keep the mind from real thoughts. A Christian meditates to sharpen thoughts.

Now the yoga question. Yoga can be taught in a variety of ways, some of which involve just exercise in balance, stretching, and general strength building. Other types of yoga training are intended to fill a spiritual void by drawing participants into the worldview of oneness and spiritual power. Therefore, if you are interested in yoga as exercise, ask questions of the instructors about their goals for the yoga training. Personally, I reject the viewpoint I sometimes hear that the body postures themselves in yoga are the channels for demonic invasion. Any exercise method involves body positions that are the same or very similar to yoga postures. I suspect that Satan does not work through chants, ceremonies, Halloween costumes, and body postures as much as through ordinary American TV commercials and self-righteousness in our churches. What your mind is up to is the essential question to ask in any question of sacred versus secular activities. Find yourself a yoga exercise class designed only to improve your balance and general strength, and you will be fine.

A Summary of Pantheism

The word *pantheism* means "everything is god" (pan: everything; theism: god). To the pantheist, however, god is not a personal God (therefore, I did not capitalize the word *god*) but an impersonal force or spirit. This worldview is also called pantheistic monism because the oneness of the cosmos is composed of only spiritual or nonphysical stuff (as opposed to the atheist's materialistic monism—all is physical stuff). The word *panpsychism* (everything is mind or soul) also has been used to describe reality for the pantheist. Mind or soul to the pantheist does not mean a personal mind like ours but an impersonal force.

The pantheistic view of human nature is that Atman (the soul of the human being) is Brahman (the soul of the universe). Pantheistic ultimate reality is one, undifferentiated spirit. This means that no one thing exists. There are no separate objects or personalities. Anything that apparently exists as a separate, distinct object is an illusion. This ultimate oneness means that human beings do not exist. We are one with the universe. We are not becoming one, but we are one. Atman is Brahman.

The path to oneness of being is to realize one's oneness with the cosmos and thus pass beyond personality. This is the end of the self-illusion. As with atheism, this worldview does not explain human nature as much as it explains it away. The religious exercises of Eastern religions are not religious at all in the sense of relating humans to God, but are more like techniques to screen out sensory input or to dissolve thinking processes. The eyes (and the other senses) are closed and the mantra, which is chanted or focused upon, helps reduce thought to nothing. Thus sensory input and internal reasoning disappear along with the feelings of self they help create. Oneness is the loss of self and ego boundaries and a joining with the universal soul.

To realize oneness is to go beyond categories of good and evil. There is no longer any basis in the pantheistic worldview for ethics or right and wrong in decision making. There are no bad people who may some day become good people, because time and behavior are illusions. No behaviors, no flow of time, and no change of character exist in pantheism. All is perfect or good; the words become meaningless to us at this point in a pantheistic discussion of ethical behavior. Ordinary ways of expressing truth or evidence are obviously meaningless in pantheism.

Suffering is also an illusion in pantheism. There is no real person struggling with cancer, hoping to be cured in the future. The sick and the well are all one. The broken leg and the healthy leg are the same. All is an illusion. Death ends the personal illusion but not the union with Brahman.

The greatest flaw in the pantheistic worldview is that by its own admission it passes no test of evidence or logic since it views the world and self-reflection as unreal. Therefore, this worldview becomes unlivable. One must ignore the entire world of sensory experience and thought as illusory, and trust in a oneness experience that a person cannot recall having and cannot communicate to others. Pantheism gives its serious spiritual seekers a long, lonely search with little hope of success. It is an unlivable worldview (Who can possibly live as if the world is an illusion and all things around us are not here?) that ends up being lived out instead as Hinduism and Buddhism in the East and the New Age movement in the West.

To summarize, the pantheistic worldview believes that reality is merely one spirit (or "force," a word popularized in the *Star Wars* films, might be a better word). There are no things or beings in the universe. All is one. So, too, Atman is Brahman—the soul of the human being is the soul of the universe. Therefore, there are no values, no purpose, and no meaning to life. There is no suffering, no disease, and no war. All things are an unchanging oneness. All else is an illusion.

The Worldview of Pantheism: Nonpersons

BELIEFS	PANTHEISM
REALITY	**Pantheism, panpsychism:** Means all is one god or, better stated, all is one mind or spirit (not a personal mind or spirit, however). **Reality, time, and individuality are illusions.**
KNOWLEDGE	**There is no knowledge but oneness and "un-knowing":** Knowing is getting beyond self as distinct from anything else. Knowledge is transcending self and body and the awareness of thoughts, feelings, and goals. This is anti-knowledge, anti-senses, and anti-feelings.
HUMAN NATURE	**Atman is Brahman:** The soul of the person is the soul of the universe. This is the same as saying you are not here. You are one with the universe. You are not "becoming one," but you are one. There is no "you." If you can recall having a oneness experience, then you really did not have one, because "you" would not have been there to experience it. Therefore, these truths cannot be taught but only searched after by each individual.
HUMAN PROBLEMS	**Human problems do not really exist:** They are just illusions. **Self-perception is the problem:** Your senses are deceiving you. There is no world out there. Your feelings of self and problems are incorrect. Meditate and you and your problems will disappear.
SOLUTIONS TO HUMAN PROBLEMS	**Meditate and your problems will disappear:** You must screen out sensory or mental inputs with meditation or other similar techniques. The technique is not necessarily religious. You can dim sensory and self feelings by biofeedback, hallucinogenic drugs, floating in water for hours, or any one of a number of other techniques.

BELIEFS	PANTHEISM
HUMAN VALUE	**All things are equally valuable or of no value:** Value statements are meaningless statements to the pantheistic worldview. I can say, "I love you." But when I follow with, "I love pencils, I love dirt, I love illness, I love dog hair," then you know that my declaration of love for you is meaningless.
HUMAN PURPOSE	**To become one with the universe:** To achieve oneness and lose this erroneous sense of self.
ETHICS	**None. No one way is better than any other.** You are both sinner and saint. You are not a bad person slowly becoming better, but you are all things now. It is meaningless to talk about your bank robberies or acts of kindness, because none of those exist. All is one.
SUFFERING	**Suffering is not real:** Your heart attack is only part of the world of illusion. Neither does your broken heart exist.
MEANING OF LIFE	**No meaning or overarching story:** There is no passage of time where you change or become better. There is no goal to reach or message or purpose to live out. All is one time and space now. You are one with all.
HUMAN DESIRE	**Desire is painful, to be eradicated:** Desire makes you form self-awareness and reflect on self. Meditation helps you eliminate self-thoughts, any thoughts, and any perceptions.

I HAVE A QUESTION

Can you redefine panpsychism and the phrase "Atman is Brahman"? I understand them when I read them, but then ten seconds later I forget what they are.

We learn things by repetition, so let me repeat often. Panpsychism is another word for pantheism. The "psychism" part shows our Western reluctance to use the word theism, which means god. We have been atheists or agnostics too long in the West to use the word *god*. The word *psychism* comes from the word for mind, and it shows up in our word *psychology*. Let me throw out some negatives in order to help you see the meaning of panpsychism. The universe is not made up of little atoms or big planets or billions of people and angels. The universe is just a unified spiritual form with no discreteness or separateness at all. This means there is no God talking to a human being. There is no love of a man for a woman. There is no time passing. There is no change from bad to better. There is no separateness in the universe, only unity. Anything else is illusion.

"Atman is Brahman" means essentially that you are not here; you do not exist as a separate person, separate from cows, crows, or other persons. Atman (you) is Brahman (the oneness spirit of the universe).

It is hard for me to believe in a worldview that gets rid of me in spite of all of my feelings and observations to the contrary.

Testing Pantheism

Remember that a true pantheist is not going to be trusting his senses for corroborating evidences or depending upon logic for testing a worldview. He is going to be sitting cross-legged and meditating on nothingness. The pantheist fails the first two tests of a worldview by refusing to take them. The third test, that of existential repugnance, however, is taken by everyone, whether willingly or not. The worldview of pantheism fails on all three tests.

The Test of Evidence

Pantheism fails this test because the world is here and can be measured in the presence of witnesses. The pantheist would say in his defense that the world is an illusion, albeit a persistent illusion, to be dispelled as you meditate and make it disappear. In favor of his case, he is able to occasionally feel a loss of sense of body and self when he is meditating, especially when he can screen out almost all sensory input. But why is this illusion of world and self so persistent? Babies are born into this illusion without any teaching from us. Trained meditators, even after a lifetime of experiencing bits and pieces of oneness experiences, still remain self-consciously in the world of things and people. The third test, the test of existential repugnance, makes it impossible to deny the evidence of our senses and personal experiences.

The Test of Logical Consistency

The pantheist would say that the only true test of a worldview is illogic: only when a thing and its opposite are both true, are we in the presence of truth. This is an unbelievable denial of the law of noncontradiction. It is both raining and not raining at the same time, says the pantheist. Actually the pantheistic worldview passes the test of logical consistency when it says, "All in the universe is one. A human being is a part of the universe. Therefore a human being is one with the universe." But the pantheist would rather be marked down as a failure on this test because of refusal to submit to it. Certainly pantheism fails to think through and admit the importance of this test for daily living. That comment brings us to the "daily living" test of existential repugnance.

The Test of Existential Repugnance

This test eventually catches everyone who holds a faulty worldview. It is nice to say all is one, persons do not exist, and all is illusion, but no one can live out this belief system. Why, then, would anyone think it is true? Everyone on the planet—pantheist, theist, and atheist—lives as if the world is real and that life does matter. Pantheists cross busy streets just like everyone else. They look out for the big buses just like everyone else. Pantheists walk through doorways and sit in chairs. They avoid angry dogs, they pull flies out of their hamburgers, and they expect to be treated fairly. Yes, there may be a stubborn pantheist somewhere who is sitting on a bed of nails in the mountains of India freezing to death in the snow because none of that exists. But such a person is soon dead and no longer contributes to the debate.

We cannot prove that the world is real and is here, but there is no need to become a skeptic or a rigid atheist because of that. We can prove few things in life. Yet most of us on the planet live as if we can trust our senses, as if persons exist, as if communication is possible, and as if people should communicate truly and act fairly toward other human beings. In fact, that is the way almost all people throughout history have lived their lives. I see no reason to doubt this test of evidence. If you cannot live out your worldview or conceive of it being lived out in the human order, then why believe it?

I HAVE A QUESTION

The major point I missed in these last few paragraphs was the "law of noncontradiction." You may have mentioned it before, but what is it?

Sorry. I guess I was just rushing along to make my point. The law of noncontradiction says that opposites cannot both be true, at least not in ordinary human living. (In particle physics that is a different matter, but you are not living in the subatomic world.) Logically we expect reality to be "either/or." Either you are here, or you are not. Either you have cancer, or you do not have cancer, and it is important to find out. There is a reality, even if I do not know what it is. The pantheist is saying all is one—past, present, and future—essentially denying any reality as we know it. To me it seems existentially repugnant to live without knowing whether you are driving on the wrong side of the road. Six billion people on the planet actively live in the world of sensory information and logic, no matter what their worldview preaches.

SOME TERMS TO THINK ABOUT

Brahman. A Hindu word meaning the stuff of all reality, the spirit underlying all reality. The *Star Wars* films use the word *force,* which is a good definition.

cosmic consciousness. The oneness experience during successful meditation exercises. Those who experience this say they are more in tune with the spiritual vibrations of the universe and feel a oneness with things around them.

meditation. This is a technique to help a person screen out sensory input in order to lower one's perception of self and reality. Often it involves closing your eyes and concentrating on a single nonsense sound like the mantra "ommmm." Without the mind engaged or the senses enabled, the person composed of only sensory input begins to disappear according to the pantheist. Of course you can just meditate as a Christian on a specific thought about God or life and thus have clearer thought and more peace in life.

om. A favorite mantra on which to meditate in pantheism. Om itself has no meaning and nothing to create thought or emotion. Thus the mind is emptied, and then oneness and absence of personal reflection can occur. To meditate on "my car has a flat tire" has so much content and emotion that the mind is filled and not emptied.

pantheism. Everything is god with a small *g*. This is not a belief in a personal God, or spirit, or mind. Again your personhood becomes an impediment to believing in this worldview.

ELEVEN

The New Age Movement

A "Street" Version of Pantheism

It is true that we have really in Flatland a Third unrecognized Dimension called "height," just as it is also true that you have really in Spaceland a Fourth unrecognized Dimension called by no name at present, but which I will call "extra height."

EDWIN A. ABBOTT

PANTHEISM, WITH ITS BELIEF that reality is an illusion, is not a worldview that can be lived out by materialistic, Western human beings. A livable alternative is found in the New Age movement. The puzzle-box picture for the New Age movement worldview shows an exciting world of people and culture and a source of power shining from above, infusing them with life. I see Americans driving their fast cars, eating rich foods, and then heading off to their twenty-minute, Eastern meditation sessions.

The New Age movement worldview represents an attempt to make Eastern pantheism more acceptable and livable to Western culture. Western naturalism has given us a mechanical human being with no purpose or meaning to existence. Eastern pantheism, on the other hand, offers a spirit to infuse all life. The New Age movement attempts to add some spiritual potential to Western, atheistic, agnostic, or humanistic lives by offering some power and

Epigraph. Edwin A. Abbott, *Flatland: A Romance of Many Dimensions* (New York: Barnes and Noble, 1963), xii.

a future beyond physical death. But the New Age worldview leaves out sin, hell, and early Sunday morning services. Since the 1960s in the United States, a variety of spiritual offerings have appeared as the menu of the New Age movement. These offerings include transcendental meditation, psychedelic drugs, water "womb" tanks, soul travel, biofeedback, holistic medicine, pyramid power, crystal power, and reincarnation studies.

A Summary of the New Age Movement

Unlike pantheism, the New Age worldview believes that the individual self exists and that it contains all truth and power if only we could unleash it. The self is a product of a physical and spiritual evolution that will allow us to survive death and even become gods of a sort. No god exists, but self does, and each self must grow into a greater conscious awareness, into a greater subjectivity in which imagination constructs reality. The New Age movement also speaks guardedly about the presence in the universe of spiritual guides to help us in our search.

The cosmos is both a visible universe and an invisible universe of energy and being. Our limited brains function to restrict incoming reality to the physical, and we end up unaware of ultimate reality and our potential to participate in it and shape it. The core experience of the New Age movement is cosmic consciousness in which ordinary categories of space and time disappear. Cosmic consciousness is a unity experience of the oneness and unity of all life—a loss of rigid self-boundaries. All human problems eventually stem from an ignorance of our true potential, which can be unleashed in cosmic awareness.

In the New Age movement, physical death is not the end of the self, or soul. One popular option for the afterlife is reincarnation, a progression of existences, hopefully upward toward cosmic existence. In the spiritual reality of the New Age, there also exist spirit beings who act as guides and possess powers to hurt or to heal.

The New Age universe is not just matter. It takes on an animistic, almost divine form as spiritual energy.

I HAVE A QUESTION

Where do New Age people get their certainty that this worldview accurately depicts the way things are?

That's a good question to ask of any worldview. Understand first of all that most people you meet who hold a particular worldview have not put a lot of thought into why they think their worldview is correct. Most postmodern people, including those who hold the New Age worldview, have experiences and feelings that contribute to their view of what is true. For some, truth may come from the altered states of consciousness experienced in meditation. For others, knowledge might come from faint memories of another life. For many, the choice of a pantheistic worldview is a relative choice. One can choose any religious viewpoint one wants, and the New Age worldview fills an inner desire to find a spiritual future instead of the dead-end grave.

The New Age movement, however, has not delivered a new age. There is no transcendent God to be the source for human personality, nor is there an ethical foundation in the absolute character of God to guide human behavior. At its best, the New Age movement looks like rich Americans playing with religion. At its worst, the New Age movement becomes an occultic experience, a dabbling in things demonic. Thus, life to millions of Americans involved in the New Age movement remains unfulfilled and spiritually sterile.

However, the appearance of the New Age movement is actually closer to Christian theism than the pantheism that spawned it. We human beings *are* spiritual as well as physical beings. There *are* spiritual beings out there in the universe. We *are* in a lesser state than our potential would indicate. Christianity *does* teach that we are destined through Christ to become glorious children of God and corulers of the universe with Christ. We *will* live for eternity as individual selves but in the unity of the body of Christ. There is a New Age to come, but it will only come through the God who became a human being in order to save us.

The Worldview of the New Age Movement: Hollow Persons

BELIEFS	NEW AGE MOVEMENT
REALITY	**There is an underlying oneness and common spirit to all things and beings.** **There are spiritual beings out there.** These beings can act as helpers and guides to your search. **Matter and self coexist with this oneness.**
KNOWLEDGE	**Knowledge comes in part from experiencing altered states of consciousness.** **Meditation:** Screening out all sensory input until oneness experiences become part of your individual being. **Human experience:** Human feelings are knowledge. **Sensory experience:** Empiricism can teach us about the physical world.
HUMAN NATURE	**Humans are highly evolved beings of spiritual power.** **Self is a future god.**
HUMAN PROBLEMS	**To be unaware of one's spiritual power**
SOLUTIONS TO HUMAN PROBLEMS	**Achieve more harmony by being in contact with the spiritual force of the universe**
HUMAN VALUE	**High value as potentially powerful spiritual beings**
HUMAN PURPOSE	**To evolve to spiritual reality and power** **Cosmic consciousness:** The experience of oneness, of loss of sense of self.

BELIEFS	NEW AGE MOVEMENT
ETHICS	**Relativism:** Ethical choices are up to the individual. **Human experience is the guide:** Inner feelings tell one of the rightness or wrongness of behavior.
SUFFERING	**Low level of awareness:** When the people do not realize their inner, spiritual potential to cure disease, avoid misfortune, or create the reality to fulfill all their desires.
MEANING IN LIFE	**All life is flowing, evolving toward a point of full potential for human life.**
HUMAN DESIRE	**All humans desire inner peace and oneness within self and with the universe:** Through meditation and other techniques you can discover the power to fulfill those deep desires you experience.

Testing the New Age Movement

When I gave subtitles to secular humanism and the New Age movement, I called them "street versions," or livable versions, of a worldview. These are the worldviews that people are living in the streets in the real world. They are not just academic theories. It is impossible to live out naturalism, which leaves us with no meaning, purpose, or value to life. But secular humanism avoids that painful belief by ignoring the logic of its own system and accepting the obvious richness of the human personality on the basis of feelings. It then becomes the worldview we see on the street. In real life we all live as if there is some meaning and value to our lives. It is difficult, if not impossible, to do otherwise.

Similarly, we will not meet any true pantheists, because they do not believe in communicating, eating, holding jobs, or marrying. The people we meet who hold pantheistic ideas also believe in the real world and themselves, but they avoid the messy belief in a God who holds people responsible for their actions. The New Age movement is thus a "street" version of the very unlivable pantheistic worldview.

The New Ager is living as if all is not one, as if there is spirit and spiritual power out there, and as if we all need to have some sort of spiritual life. As Christians we agree there is a spiritual world, a spiritual God and angels, and a spiritual potential within us. But there is nothing other than a weak parade of evidence to tell us how we are evolving toward this potential, or who the spirit guides are, or why pyramids and crystals focus spiritual power.

The New Age worldview passes the test of evidence, fails the test of logical consistency, and passes the test of existential repugnance.

The Test of Evidence

The New Age movement does not work seriously at gathering evidence for the nature of its proposed spiritual realities and goals. ESP studies and reincarnation testimonies are about as scientific as it gets. But I will generously give it a passing grade, because the New Age worldview does draw attention to spiritual possibilities. Atheism left us with a material world and no personhood or value for ourselves. That is a bleak viewpoint. The worldview of pantheism does the opposite, saying there is only spirit and it is everywhere and in all things and is all things. If reality is neither all matter (atheism) nor all spirit (pantheism), we need a worldview that can hold both matter and spirit together. The New Age sees that need and suggests that somehow the spirit of the universe is alive and well within us. We will see that Christian theism teaches that both matter and spirit exist and it is in the middle ground of human beings as created by our God where matter and spirit join. Indeed, God Himself entered the world of matter as a person. God is the center of the Christian theistic worldview, and we will turn to that in the next chapter.

The Test of Logical Consistency

The New Age worldview suffers from the same problem as the atheistic, Western worldviews. Where is the basis for personhood in this worldview? What in the impersonal universal spirit gives value and individual personalities to human beings? The New Age worldview is not consistent with its own presuppositions.

The Test of Existential Repugnance

It is possible for people to live as if they have spiritual power and importance. But the New Age worldview looks more like bored Americans trying out something fun rather than making the hard choice of submitting to a moral and spiritual restructuring of their lives. There is no accounting for the guilt feelings and moral strivings that go beyond the "I'm on my way to the spiritual heights" teachings of the New Age movement. But, as I did for secular humanism, I will give this worldview a passing grade because many Americans live comfortably with this worldview, which gives them some hope for a future life after death.

SOME TERMS TO THINK ABOUT

New Age. The hoped for future of no pain, no war, no endless striving for happiness. All who enter this age will find happiness in the vast depth of the spiritual universe.

New Age movement. This is a livable version of the pantheistic worldview that is very popular in the United States. In the New Age movement, you can believe in your electronic toys and new clothes and still do your meditating on the weekend.

reincarnation. Taught by Eastern religions, this is the cycle of birth and death and rebirth. Life is not heading toward some spiritual heaven but is locked into this endless cycle. There is a hopelessness that affects those who believe in reincarnation because they see only the continual loss of self, and coming back as a turkey would not increase one's chances to find enlightenment the next time around.

TWELVE

Christian Theism
Personhood Explained

And that is precisely what Christianity is about. This world is a
great sculptor's shop. We are the statues and there is a rumour going
round the shop that some of us are some day going to come to life.

C. S. LEWIS

THE PUZZLE BOX YOU HAVE just been handed for Christian theism
looks similar to many of the others. There is a world of nature with
stars, flowers, and animals. There are people doing scientific and
artistic things. There is sin and war and much unhappiness. But
there is also joy and good present in the world. This box-top picture
also shows a world above the sun, a heaven in which God resides
and His light illumines the minds and lives of people. And Jesus
Christ is that God, present in history and in the lives and hearts of
those who are willing to believe in Him.

It is important to note at this point that we have examined the
major worldviews, and none of them has passed all three tests of a
worldview. We need a worldview that fits the facts, is logical, and is
livable. And that is exactly what Christian theism turns out to be.
Christian theism fits reality and human need so well that one might
claim that it was invented to meet the human need. But Christian

Epigraph. C. S. Lewis, *Mere Christianity* (New York: Macmillan, 1943), 140.

theism was not invented. The fact is, Christian theism fits reality and human nature so well because it is true.

And so we have arrived at the worldview that many readers here claim to be theirs. Christian theism is a supernaturalistic worldview that believes in a personal God who is the creator of heaven and earth and all their inhabitants. Christian theists, of course, believe that Jesus Christ is that personal God, who has entered the world of human beings. This supernaturalistic worldview does not rule out the importance of the natural realm or what we can learn from it.

We will begin this chapter with a worldview matrix that gives us a brief overview of the essentials of Christian theism. This chapter's look at Christian theism will focus largely on its view of personhood since that is where the issues with competing worldviews seem to lie. No worldview that denies personhood in human beings seems intellectually and personally satisfying to human beings, who are searching in these box tops for clues to the puzzle of life. Following this summary of Christian theism, we will see how this worldview fares with regard to the three tests of a worldview. In later chapters we will look more closely at the evidence for Christian theism and at the very difficult problem of why God allows suffering.

I HAVE A QUESTION

Whatever good things you are now about to say about the Christian worldview, is it not true that this worldview killed thousands of people in the Crusades and the Inquisition? Was it not Christian Germany that produced an Adolf Hitler, and is it not Christian America that is the pornography capital of the world? There is a lot of sin, irrational thinking, and hostile behavior bound up in your Christian worldview. Am I not correct?

You have brought up a very common objection to Christianity as a worldview and religion. Actually, we have to first separate the actions of Christians, undoubtedly a minority of Christians, from what Jesus Christ taught and lived. There are sinners in the Christian church as in any religion. In fact, it is the message of Christ that welcomes sinners into the fold, and this message often angered the very religious and "perfect" Pharisees in the New Testament. Jesus' behavior and teaching, on the other hand, went straight to the divorced woman at the well; the woman taken in adultery; Zacchaeus and Matthew, both hated tax gatherers; the Roman centurion; and more—all sinners who were saved by the grace of Jesus Christ. The Christian life is described as one of continual growth over time from our imperfect minds and lives to better thinking and living after the model of Jesus Christ's life. No one has ever claimed that the Christian life was easy or perfect.

At the same time you are thinking of the Crusades and the Inquisition, sobering examples of some Christian failures, think also of the much more numerous works of Christians in society at all periods of Christian history, in building hospitals and schools, in preventing wars, and in ministering to the poor and the sick.

The following matrix briefly lists the basic beliefs of Christian theism's worldview. Obviously it is difficult to capture the meaning of the Christian worldview, or any other worldview, with just a few words. Longer explanations on some elements here will follow in this chapter and later chapters, but the matrix does allow us to see the whole worldview and how it answers the ultimate questions of life. With these brief worldview statements, we can test and compare worldviews more easily.

The Christian Theistic Worldview: Personhood Explained

BELIEFS	CHRISTIAN THEISM
REALITY	**God exists.** **He is a person.** **The Trinity—God is three persons in one God:** God is unity and diversity at the same time, and He created a world of unity and diversity. I cannot understand this, even though I do understand much of the Christian worldview. What makes me think that I could ever comprehend the total reality of God? **Jesus Christ is God's own Son, and He is God Himself in this Trinity:** The mystery of God is reduced to a human being, whom we can see and learn from in history and in our personal lives. **God created the material universe and human beings, who are dependent upon, but separate from, God.**
KNOWLEDGE	**Special revelation in the Bible and the person of Jesus Christ** **General revelation**—the world of nature and human experience
HUMAN NATURE	**A unified physical, mental, and spiritual being** **Free will in the midst of strong influences** **Image of God**—He is a person. We are persons.
HUMAN PROBLEMS	**Fallenness (or sin nature)** **Physical and mental and cultural defects**
SOLUTIONS TO HUMAN PROBLEMS	**Change of human nature (new birth) in the gospel of Jesus Christ** **Physical and mental and cultural changes**
HUMAN VALUE	**High value declared by God**
HUMAN PURPOSE	**To give glory to God**—to reveal God's nature and character in our lives. **To do God's work in this world** **To enjoy God and His world**

BELIEFS	CHRISTIAN THEISM
ETHICS	**Absolutes in right and wrong come from the absolute character of God as revealed in the Bible and the person of Jesus Christ.**
SUFFERING	**Must be understood within God's love, power, and purpose**
MEANING IN LIFE	**History is linear, not cyclical. It is moving toward a God-ordained conclusion.** **Your life is a story and fits within a larger story by God.**
HUMAN DESIRE	**All deep desires are longings for the God of the universe and what He created us for.** **Human desires for truth, beauty, love, eternity, heroism, morality, and more are for the core of life in Jesus Christ. We were made for more than nature.**

Testing Christian Theism

How does Christian theism fair on the three tests of a worldview? As we will see, it passes all three tests.

The Test of Evidence

The Christian description of human nature above the nature of animal fits with the evidence we gather as we look at human brains, language, the arts, world religions, or our own inner desires. This is not an argument against the theory of evolution but against any worldview that explains away rather than explains human nature. Human beings seem very different from the animal world and at the same time very similar. Those differences must not be ignored. The human brain exhibits an incredible complexity that rivals any physical structure in the universe, and that brain/mind combination seems more designed to read Shakespeare than to find bananas and grass. The world's history is filled with struggles for destiny and purpose that go far beyond the survival of one's genes. Examples of genocide can more easily be explained as examples of sin nature unrestrained by cultural laws than as genes guaranteeing their own futures. The world's history is filled with literature, art, music, science, and religious devotion, all of which point to a deeper desire and nature in human beings. Yet none of this denies the physical bodies we possess or their similarity to animal bodies.

The Test of Logical Consistency

It is logically consistent to say that God is a personal, creator God and that He created human beings in His personal image. Human beings are persons, just as God is a person, with self-awareness, language, and creative and communicative abilities. Personhood does not have to be explained away with statements that we are just biological machines or animals. Personhood does not have to be explained away as illusory elements in a pantheistic oneness. The most fundamental experience of our lives and knowledge—that we are persons—cannot be denied and can be explained by the existence of a personal God, who created us in His image.

The Test of Existential Repugnance

I cannot perfectly live up to the teachings of Christ, but I can conceive of a world in which those teachings are practiced. It would seem to be a very pleasant world indeed to live as if you and all other people were valuable creatures, as if neighbor and even enemy mattered and were to be loved. It is conceivable and desirable to think of a life after death, or the end of our sorrows, or mercy for sins.

Let me now develop in a little more depth some of these Christian beliefs. We have heard these belief statements our whole lives, and yet we may fail to see or understand the reality of what they mean.

A Biblical View of the Person: Image of God

One of the dangers of describing a biblical view of the person is that the "religious" language used can make readers feel that they are reading a sermon. They may feel that what I am saying is now about church matters, and we are no longer in the same academic arena as biological and psychological descriptions of human nature. We are still talking about truth, however, but it is truth not from dissecting tables or interviews, but from the God of the universe, the One who created us.

As a psychologist I realize how enlightening this biblical perspective is in helping us to understand the *whole* of the nature of the person. Biological and psychological descriptions of the person must be complemented by the serious discussion of the human spiritual nature and purpose. This spiritual content from the creator of our beings ties together the mysteries of human nature, which are continually unveiled in our academic pursuits.

The first item to note about the biblical description of the person is that the Bible finds it impossible to talk about human nature without talking about God. Talk about God, however, seems superfluous to those who do not believe in the God of the Bible. The general attitude toward such biblical information seems to be: "just describe the person, and leave God and religion out of it." The biblical answer to that objection is that, since human beings were created to be related to God, any description of human nature that does not take into account God's creative purposes will be incomplete. A naturalist, for example, tends to approach the description of human nature in shallow, objective ways without reference to human purpose. But this may not be the best way to describe even nonpersonal objects.

What would be the best way to describe a flashlight to a person from the distant past, who knew nothing of modern flashlights? With today's naturalistic worldview we could describe a flashlight objectively as a certain quantity of plastic, glass, and battery chemicals, but that would hardly be helpful to the person from the past in our illustration. We could offer a similar objective description of the human person as consisting of so many pounds of muscle and bone, or so many neural connections, but such an objective description falls far short of the reality of persons.

Such descriptions of a flashlight or a person are incomplete and not helpful. However, to refer to purpose or function in flashlights or persons is enlightening. Turn the flashlight on, and any person suddenly knows what the flashlight is by seeing its purpose, what it was made to do. So, also, to describe the purpose of a human being is to go beyond the objective descriptions and to provide the core of what a human being is all about in God's creative will. Therefore, I want to give a description of the human person by beginning with a description of human purpose and God's image in human nature.

Human Purpose

According to the Bible and noted by our catechisms and confessions of faith, human purpose is to give glory to God. That sounds very otherworldly and religious, does it not? Giving glory to God gives one the impression of standing in a crystal cathedral, holding votive candles, and singing some Gregorian, monophonic chant. However, that image is not even close to what the Bible means by giving glory to God. Glory is an ordinary word that we use in non-religious contexts. To give glory to someone means to tell who that one is and what he or she can do. What do we mean when we call a basketball player a "glory hog"? Is there something religious about his or her behavior? Not at all. We mean that his actions on the basketball court tell us more about him than about what the team can do or what the coach's plan is. A painting gives glory to the painter, whose emotions and thoughts are revealed on the canvas. Clothes and handwriting give glory to people as well; that is, they tell us something, however little, about people's personalities.

I HAVE A QUESTION

You haven't quoted any Bible verses yet to support your ideas on the biblical view of the person, and I wonder why not. Do you have a problem with the Bible?

No, I do not have any problem with the Bible and the rich truth it brings to our lives. I know these items in the Christian worldview are supported by Bible verses, and I will bring up some relevant biblical passages as we travel further into this worldview. But what I am trying not to do at this moment is to act like biblical truth is somehow different from other ways of knowing, with the exception that the source of its information is God Himself. As I said before, as soon as we start talking about biblical truth, some people switch into another mode of thinking—like, "Aha, now we are in religious knowledge—those things you make up to explain something you don't understand." I am not ashamed of biblical truth, but I want it recognized for what it is. The Bible speaks to the same reality that concerns those in all the academic disciplines, and I must still use my mind and good interpretive skills to discover exactly what the Bible is saying to us.

That was a long answer, but I hope you can see that I am cautious of merely sprinkling Bible verses all over my book and giving a spiritual blessing to the matters at hand. Some Bible verses are about to follow, and I want you to notice that I am not "proof-texting" or just throwing a verse or two onto the table for discussion. The verses I will use summarize vast areas of biblical teaching on the subject, and I would expect that other areas of truth gathering throughout the liberal arts will bear witness to these biblical ideas.

To give glory to God is not simply a religious expression but one that says that human beings were created, like all things in the universe, to reveal something about the nature and character of God. Trees give glory to God. Worms give glory to God. The solar system gives glory to God. All aspects of the physical world can tell us something about the power, beauty, and mind of the Creator. I am not sure what a worm tells me about God's nature as opposed to what a massive black hole reveals, but both, as created objects, must reveal the activity of the Creator in their particular forms. The essence of the biblical description of the person is that God created a personal being like Himself, a created being who can actually reveal something of the personality of God Himself.

Image of God

Genesis reveals that mankind was created in God's image (Gen. 1:26–28). This "image of God" refers, in general, to the fact that God is a person and we are persons. The importance of this in our discussion of human nature is that God created a being similar to Himself and, therefore, that being can reveal more of the nature and character of God than trees and stars, which are incapable of revealing the personal characteristics of God. A five-fingered glove can reveal more of the nature of the hand within it than a two-fingered mitten because the glove is made in the image of the hand. Human beings alone are created in the image of God and, like the five-fingered glove, can reveal more fully than any other created thing, the nature of their Creator.

But human beings as persons have free will, and thus, unlike trees, they can choose to reveal their own natures rather than God's nature. The history of the world and of our own lives more often has been the revealing of our own wills than the revealing of God's character through our own character. But the description of human nature does not stop with being made in God's image in order to better reveal God's personality. The biblical description of the person also includes the possibility of inheriting life from God and becoming literally related to God as a child is to a parent.

Children of God

The New Testament description of the person includes the startling idea that God wants to give His spiritual life to human beings just as a parent gives physical, genetic life to a child. This "new birth" teaching (John 3) is not just a metaphor for getting a new start with God; it means that human beings can inherit God's spiritual "DNA" (Peter calls it spiritual "seed" in 1 Peter 1:23) and can mature and resemble Jesus Christ in character. This new life results, then, in human beings giving glory to God as they grow in the image of their Father. As they mature in Christ, they have the inherited potential to become in character like their spiritual Father (the fruit of the Spirit, Gal. 5:22–23) and thus reveal what God is like. What a remarkable view of human nature this is! We are not just bodies but persons who will for all eternity reveal the God of the universe in the way we think and feel and live.

A Biblical View of the Person: Sin Nature

A biblical view of human nature is built on two opposite pillars. One pillar, which has just been discussed, is that human beings are created in the image of God. Obviously, being related to the God of the universe is a very positive statement about human nature. But there is another pillar holding up the biblical view of human nature, and it is not positive. As important as the image of God is to an understanding of human beings, of equal importance is the fact that human nature is fallen; the original image is marred. It is this negative aspect of human nature to which we now turn.

The biblical emphasis on the fallen condition of human nature is not on humanity's bank robberies and sexual sins. The biblical emphasis is not so much that human beings are "bad," as that they are "bad off." My language suggests that the biblical emphasis is not on the bad behavior of human beings but on a nature crippled by the loss of and continued absence of a relationship with God. Paul the apostle, in his epistle to the Romans, takes this emphasis when he uses the word *sin* (singular) to mean sin nature, as opposed to the word *sins* (plural) to mean bad behavior. To Paul it is sin, not sins, which is the ultimate problem with human nature. Sins or bad behavior, which often became the preoccupation of the religious establishment in Jesus' day (as well as our own), may be the best evidence for the fallen, sin nature but not the only evidence. It is clear in Romans 1–3 that all people have a sin nature, no matter how many or few sins they have committed. This should be familiar theology to Christians, but it tends to be submerged in even the best campaigns against bad behavior. If "sins" (bad behavior) was the problem with humanity, then good behavior would be our salvation. But being saved by our good works is not New Testament teaching. If, on the other hand, "sin," or a fallen nature, is the ultimate problem with humanity, then it follows that a new nature in Christ and the power for living good lives becomes the "gospel," or good news, of salvation for all humankind.

To summarize, the emphasis of biblical revelation is not on human bad behavior but on the crippled nature of human beings, which, like a deadly disease, is lethal to real life. This view does not take away from human responsibility for sins or minimize the terrible consequences of sins that we bring upon ourselves and others; rather it focuses, just as Christ did, on the real issue. Jesus did not center on the sins of Zacchaeus or Matthew or the woman at the well or the woman taken in adultery. Instead, Jesus revealed the compassion of God for the lostness of human beings and God's stiff resistance to the legalism of the self-righteous Pharisees. The biblical account, beginning in Genesis 3, is clear that the historic fall of Adam and Eve was real in its effects on their natures and that those effects were inherited by all who were born into this state of "sin."

Obviously, I am interpreting Genesis 3 as a historical account of something that had real effects on the entirety of humanity. The Genesis 3 effects of the Fall fit the three dimensions or capabilities of human nature—the physical, the spiritual, and the mental. Let me summarize the effects of the Fall on human nature in these three areas.

One result of the fall of Adam and Eve is physical death. Today human beings are mortal and begin to die from the moment they are born. Death is a part of all life on this planet. In fact, the entire universe is cursed (the biblical word in Genesis 3) and speeds toward a state of decay. A quick glance at our bodies and the universe reminds us of the poetic groaning of all creation in the second half of Romans 8.

A second inherited consequence of the historic fall of Adam and Eve is spiritual death. If death means "separated from life," then physical death is being separated from what gives one physical life, such as oxygen and food. In the same sense, spiritual death means separation from a relationship with God, which is the only way one's deepest needs in life (the spiritual) can be met. Therefore, spiritually dead human beings will never meet their deepest needs and are forever trying to fill the void with other things, whether physical or social, with both good works and sinful behavior. Many human tears and much bad behavior are the visible outworkings of a fallen nature.

I HAVE A QUESTION

No one believes in the Devil anymore, so why turn to the Bible rather than a psychologist for understanding problems in human nature?

It may not be popular in some academic cultures to believe in spiritual beings like angels and devils, but the Bible does teach of their existence. In fact, Jesus is the primary teacher we have on the nature of spiritual beings. If we determine there is good evidence to believe the Bible for what it claims to be, God's message to us, then we need to rethink what we believe about evil beings in our world. This is not to say that mental illness is the product of demons, but neither is it to say that demon possession or Satan's activity in the world is not true. As a Christian psychologist, I believe that there are many factors, including the biological, behavioral, cultural, and spiritual that can affect one's mental health.

A third effect of the Fall involves the personal-social dimension of human life. This result of the Fall could be called, not selfishness, but "self-centeredness." The Genesis 3 language of Adam and Eve's "eyes being opened" and "becoming like God" seems to mean that they began to see reality from their own perspective, that is, they became the center of their own experience and existence, rather than God being at the center of their lives. While we cannot know what Adam and Eve's pre-fallen experience was like, it is clear that after the Fall they, and everyone born after them, seemed bent inward on self and prone to selfishness, isolation, and an emptiness of soul. The New Testament language of growth in faith, love, and oneness with each other seems to be a reversal over time of this great human isolation and emptiness.

What the fall of human nature into sin means practically speaking is that while human beings are possessed of a great potential and desire from the image of God in them, at the same time, they are incapable of reaching this potential and happiness. Therefore, we lapse continually and easily into moments and lifetimes of sin and sorrow. It is no mystery and no embarrassment to ourselves to admit in the face of such a tragic situation that our only hope is in God, who cares for us and is capable of helping us.

SOME TERMS TO THINK ABOUT

God. God is a person, and He has a personal name. His name is YHWH (the tetragrammaton), the four unpronounceable letters. When we want to pronounce it, we say Yahweh or Jehovah, religious scholars' attempts to insert vowels. The Old Testament Jews decided to put another word, *Adonai*, meaning "Lord," in its place when they had to pronounce the name of God.

revelation. A word that refers to the Bible, God's revealing of His message to human beings. Questions naturally arise about how this revelation was delivered and maintained for several thousand years, about interpreting it in different cultures and different times, and about alleged errors and the authorship of God. Good sources exist for assisting you on all these questions.

sin nature. Paul often uses the singular word *sin* to refer to sin nature or our crippled natures. Human beings enter the world, bent or broken or damaged, regardless of whether they have committed few sins or many sins.

sins. Used in the plural this word refers to human beings' "bad" behavior and is our best evidence for the sin nature, that something has gone dreadfully wrong with the beings God created.

to give glory to God. Refers to revealing of God's nature through our lives. God is love. Do we reveal His love to the world? If so, then we are giving glory to God.

Trinity. This seems impossible to understand, three persons in one God. But what makes us think that the ultimate truth about the God of the universe would be completely understandable to us? What is remarkable is that so much of the world of the spiritual is understandable through the revelation of God in the Bible and Jesus Christ, our God made visible.

Part 3

THE CHRISTIAN WORLDVIEW

Christianity Meets Life

I am the way and the truth and the life. (John 14:6)
JESUS

I USED TO BELIEVE THAT discovering truth in spiritual matters was a stroke of blind luck at best. We are not blind to the material world, but we are blind to any assumed world beyond the physical, I thought. How can we see into spiritual matters if all we have to search with are retinas, basilar membranes, and Pacinian corpuscles, full-fledged mysteries of sense perception themselves. I recall seeing a cartoon of Winnie the Pooh staring perplexedly at a stuffed Winnie-the-Pooh doll in his paws. The caption asked how Pooh Bear could ever understand pooh bear if he only has his Pooh brain with which to work? So, too, imagine human beings trying to understand the mysteries of human beings with nothing but human brains with which to work. How can we expect to understand spiritual things if we cannot even understand ourselves? What can mere human beings with material brains possibly know about a world beyond sensory experience? What can we possibly know with our limited senses about absolutes in morality, life after death, or the existence of a supreme being?

The agnostic cries out, "Give it up. One can never know such deep things." I was an agnostic by laziness and default when I entered graduate study in psychology more than thirty years ago. I was raised in a Catholic family. I attended Catholic schools from first grade through college, and I am sure I believed in God and the Christian faith at some level. When I left home for graduate school, I fell into agnosticism. How could anyone ever know for sure if God existed or which God was the correct one? All we could do, I thought, was to live the best life we could and obey the Golden Rule.

Imagine goldfish in a fishbowl sitting next to your color TV set. Goldfish have good color vision and presumably can focus on the nearby TV screen showing the Super Bowl football game. Those goldfish are at the top of their evolutionary tree limb in terms of their visual capabilities. But what could such goldfish possibly know about what is going on in all the splash of color and movement on the TV screen? What could they know of the twenty-two men on the field, all with hopes and dreams based on the outcome of this game? What could the goldfish possibly know about the rules of play? How could they understand that the movement on the TV screen is actually happening a thousand miles away? So, too, what makes us human beings, the peak of the animal kingdom according to most, think that we can be any closer to the truth of God or spiritual matters than goldfish are to what they see on the TV screen? We have fine brains, but the spiritual realities are far beyond us. With such safe, skeptical reasoning I was content to sleep in on Sunday mornings and wake late to leisurely read the Sunday funnies. No legalistic church service with suit and tie was to be in my life.

No person has ever invented a "spirit" scope to peer into the realms of the spirit so that we might know what is going on. But that fact does not rule out the possibility that the God of the universe could cross the chasm of unknowing from His side to our side. No spirit scopes are needed. Ordinary investigations into history and life are sufficient, if God has invaded our planet. Christianity teaches that God pierced the veil separating humanity from knowing God and entered the human world. God inspired a book in human language. God became a man and entered our world, ate our food, spoke our language, cried our tears, and experienced our death.

That same God of the universe reached out to my personal universe in perhaps the only way I would pay attention, through a dating relationship. Back in the early 1970s at Purdue University I was a graduate student minding my own business when I met a girl minding her own business, but God had other plans for both of us. She had broken her engagement with another student just before I met her. The distraught suitor left school and, through his parents' influence, eventually found a relationship with Jesus Christ. When he returned to school many months later with his newfound faith, his former fiancée and I were dating seriously. He shared his new faith with her, and she believed. She shared her new faith with me and wanted the same new life for me.

What was I supposed to do? I had been dating a normal woman who had never said a religious word since I met her, and now suddenly she was expressing belief in personal salvation through Jesus Christ. I could not believe what was happening, and I could not believe in her Jesus. We talked for hours, trying to decide whether I was a Christian or not, and we finally decided that I was not. I had not trusted Jesus Christ for my salvation. Whenever I shared with her some of the errors or inconsistencies I felt were in the Bible, she would just cry. But I could not shake her faith in her personal relationship with Jesus Christ.

One of my friends suggested that I find some books describing Christianity and use them to show her the problems with her faith. I located a Christian bookstore near campus called the Upper Room. I marched upstairs (of course) looking to find a sales clerk who would recommend books to convince my girlfriend of the errors of Christianity. Whoever that clerk was, he must have silently chuckled as he sold me Francis Schaeffer's *Escape From Reason*, Paul Little's *Know Why You Believe*, and C. S. Lewis's *Mere Christianity*. Little did I suspect the attack that those books would mount against me during the next few days.

Near the Thanksgiving holiday, I found myself reading these

books on Christianity and feeling the impending crisis I was about to face. I was a scientist finding out that Christianity had enough evidence to satisfy even me, if I was willing to believe. I read *Escape from Reason*, but I found the ideas difficult, and I did not plan on working that hard at this search. Next, I read from an author unknown to me, C. S. Lewis. I was so impressed and almost frightened to read something so bright and convincing in its description of Christianity and reasons to believe. Finally, I read Paul Little's modern classic and collapsed like a tent in the wind. Little's book answered the exact questions with which I had been challenging my girlfriend. I became academically convinced of the truth of Christianity. I believed and felt my control over my life slipping away.

One of my non-Christian friends, who knew of my distress over my girlfriend, suggested I read the Bible or New Testament to see for myself its worthlessness. I bought a paperback New Testament, and fortunately its paraphrase was helpful to me as I read parts of the Gospels. The voice of God seemed to burn in my mind as I read. It was all true, and I would be a fool to ignore it and let my mind cloud over again. I did not want to be a Christian, to go to church, to be a missionary, but I could not ignore the truth. I had not spent enough time to answer every question, but I had seen enough. My mind had required and had received evidence, but I could clearly feel that I had to be willing to believe, to open my mind, before I could believe. I did believe one night during the Thanksgiving season. As best I knew how, I accepted Jesus Christ into my heart, barely understanding what I was doing, reluctantly surrendering, expecting the worst in my new faith and lifestyle to come.

That is how Jesus Christ and Christianity met me and my life. My girlfriend and I never did get married, but our lives continued down different, God-directed paths. I learned many more evidences for my faith. I asked more questions. I married, had children, experienced a massive brain aneurysm and a miracle of surgery. I make decisions every day that spring from my new life in Jesus Christ and my faith worldview.

The next three chapters continue our discussion about Christian theism in the real world. In some ways these chapters parallel my journey and the journey of many Christians. Chapter 13 deals with the evidences, certainties, and uncertainties concerning the truth of the Christian world and life view. Christians are open to the academic challenge to their faith, and I live teaching in such an arena in my Christian university. Chapter 14 begins a discussion on suffering, perhaps the greatest challenge to the Christian view of God. My discussion is brief and only one view, but I am demonstrating that we Christians do think about this issue, as well as live with suffering and a God who loves us. Chapter 15 is about Christianity meeting the world in our lives. I have not said everything there is to be said in these last three chapters, but my point will have been made: Christians are people of a reasoned and living faith.

I HAVE A QUESTION

Well, it's not a question exactly. Thanks for sharing your personal experience of finding faith in Jesus Christ. With all these chapters you seemed like such a rational mind, sort of like Mr. Spock in Star Trek. No offense. It's nice to know there is emotion and feeling in your faith too.

Thanks. I'll take the Mr. Spock comparison as a compliment. Each one of us needs a good measure of both reason and emotion for a strong faith.

THIRTEEN

The Evidence for Christian Theism

It is improbable that anyone thought up, last week, a question that will bring Christianity crashing. Brilliant minds have probed through the profound questions of every age and have ably answered them.

PAUL E. LITTLE

IN THE PAST FEW YEARS, I have worked many Sunday mornings in our church's nursery. There I have helped small two- and three-year-old children put together five- to ten-piece puzzles. I can do a puzzle that size without a thought about what the pieces make. A bigger puzzle with hundreds or thousands of pieces needs a box-top picture. When you start on your big puzzle, how do you know you have the correct box top? Undoubtedly, you trust the puzzle companies and for many good reasons. But what if the puzzle companies were unreliable? What if several box-top pictures came with each puzzle? What would you do? You would not just pick a picture and hope it fit the pieces inside the box. That would waste your time as you tried one picture after another, with each new attempt following a big failure in the puzzle building.

Epigraph. Paul E. Little, *Know Why You Believe*, 4th ed. (Downers Grove, Ill.: InterVarsity, 2000), 20.

As puzzle builders we could use several strategies to determine which picture best fit our initial examination of the puzzle pieces. For example, are there colors in some of the puzzle pieces that are not in some of the pictures? Are there peculiar details in some of the pictures for which we can find no puzzle pieces during a brief survey of the pieces? Such testing to pick the correct puzzle box top is the same idea we have in mind when we test any worldview. We cannot waste our one life randomly putting together life's pieces, hoping it all works. We have only a small number of years in one very important life—our own. We need to decide which worldview is most likely to be correct and the one that we can base our lives and destiny upon. Therefore, a wise person tests worldviews and makes a decision to live by.

Let us briefly explore how Christian theism fairs with the first test of a worldview, the test of evidence. I cannot cover the legion of evidences in Christian apologetics, but I will surface some important ways of thinking about this whole topic. The entire area of Christian apologetics, or arguments and evidences for the Christian faith, is well established and would more than challenge anyone's searching mind. These include arguments for the existence of God and the possibility of miracles. One can read at great length on the evidences for the resurrection, the deity of Christ, the reliability of the biblical documents, and the accuracy of biblical prophecy. Legions of books have been written on archaeology and the Bible, Bible and science questions, the origin of the biblical materials, and the biblical Canon (the books included in the Bible).

One can study at length on key religious problems, such as why God allows suffering and evil, the existence of other religions, and human freedom versus God's divine will. One excellent, small book that covers the basic objections people raise about Christianity is Paul Little's classic *Know Why You Believe*, the source book for this chapter's title quote. Little's book answers in brief chapters questions such as, Has the Bible changed over the years? Are miracles possible? What about the pagan, who has never heard of the gospel of salvation? Was Jesus Christ God?

Another area deserving mention in Christian apologetics is the evidence of Christian testimony, that is, Christians who say Jesus Christ and the truth of the gospel message changed their lives. One can find nearly anywhere in the world, during all time periods since the time of Christ, people of all ages, education, and backgrounds who will stand up and testify to amazing changes in their lives because of Jesus their Savior. Any religion or belief, no matter how idiotic, can provide testimonies to its truthfulness. Testimony does not "prove" any idea or religion to be correct. Christian theism's testimonies, though, seem remarkable in comparison to those of other religions, especially in their scope.

The origins of Christianity are a case in point of remarkable evidence for the truth of Christianity's claims. Christianity should not have gotten off the ground with its leader dead on the cross. The original small Christian sect had no army, and no dominating philosophy, and its members faced years of persecution. The original leaders of the Christian movement, almost to a man, gave their lives in martyrdom to testify to the truth of Jesus Christ and their new lives in Him.

When all the studies are done, it is amazing how good the case for Christianity is. Christian theism is a rational, highly defensible world and life view. The case for Christianity may be excellent, but even so it does not necessarily leave one at the 100-percent level of certainty. We are limited human beings, and the questions and issues are complex. Still, just because some things are not perfectly clear about our Christian faith, we do not need to retreat into total uncertainty and doubt. In fact, our faith can grow with our study in the areas of our uncertainties. We need to be always on guard that static creeds do not become our primary defense against things we fail to understand.

If Christian truth is so defensible and rational, why, then, do not more people believe because of the evidence? One reason might be that a single issue, such as the problem of why God allows suffering, overshadows all the other evidences. A person might accept the clear case for Christianity from many evidences but be unable to accept a God who seemingly is so uncaring about suffering. At times there may be a moral issue or behavior at stake. The evidence for Christianity is reasonably clear, but a moral decision in the opposite direction can cloud the thinking about the evidences. A young woman living with her boyfriend may unconsciously distort the evidences for Christianity so that she does not have to deal with challenges to her moral choices. Sometimes disbelief comes down to the fact that people often believe what they want to believe in spite of evidences. Believing requires, first of all, a willingness to believe.

Another reason for lack of belief today may be the reality that people simply do not want to *think* about such personal issues as faith and morality. People want to believe that the discovery of such truth is a personal, but not a rational, choice. In such cases it is not the rational apologetic that will catch the non-believer's attention, but perhaps the very important evidence of human love and Christian life during ordinary and extraordinary life struggles that beset us all.

I HAVE A QUESTION

What about evolution and the Bible? Hasn't evolution sort of been proven, and doesn't that throw the Bible out?

This is certainly a common question people bring up today, and I do not have the room here to answer everything about your question. Let me give a general answer that can be a guide to you as you think and read about evolution. The theory of evolution refers to the development of complex animals and human beings from simpler animal forms. This theory first put forth by Charles Darwin in 1859 has run afoul of many Christians' views on how God created the world and human beings.

There are at least two major Christian views on the subject. Creationists believe that God created human beings in a special creative act. Theistic evolutionists, on the other hand, believe that God used evolution to produce what He wanted human and animal forms to be and that He is responsible for creating the immortal human souls. All Christians find it unacceptable to believe in atheistic evolution, that is, a beautiful world and a wonderful you happened without any help from a supreme being. Christians agree that God is the source of our nature, value, and purpose as human beings. How He created is what is debated among Christians. Let us not "burn at the stake" Christians with whom we disagree on this subject of creation versus evolution. Search for answers in the light of open minds seeking knowledge. Don't be quick to shut off the lights and the mind while fellow believers share their different views on the same questions.

The Apologetic from Desire

There are many arguments for supernaturalism, or the Christian worldview, and one of the most powerful in my opinion is the "apologetic from desire." This refers to the argument for Christian theism (or supernaturalism) from the evidence of the deep desires of the human heart. This apologetic explores the last belief I have listed for each worldview, that is, how a worldview explains deep human desire. How does any worldview explain the human longing for truth, beauty, justice, courage, truth, honor, heroism, morality, romance, and much more? All of these desires are seen clearly in our mass production down through the ages of literature, art, music, and now film, making public the innermost longings and deepest needs of human beings.

Let me summarize the apologetic from desire. Human beings long for more than the natural realm. Therefore, we are either freaks in the universe, or the universe is not merely a natural place. Either we are dressed in tuxes and prom dresses when there is nothing to attend but a barn dance, or we are fit for a dance with the King of the universe. In other words, we are either absurdly deep creatures in a flat universe, or the universe is as deep as we seem to be. Either we are freaks, creatures who have evolved complex abilities and desires that are not needed, or the universe is a place that fits our deepest longings for eternity, morality, love, and more. Christians take the latter option, refusing to call the dominant creature on the globe an evolutionary freak. Therefore, the world must be a supernatural place, where our deepest longings find their source and satisfaction in the God of truth, beauty, love, eternity, virtue—all that we long for.

C. S. Lewis was converted to supernaturalism and then Christianity by this apologetic from desire, as well as other evidences, as you can read in his spiritual autobiography, *Surprised by Joy*. He used the word *joy* in the title to refer to the inner desire for truth and perfection. Interestingly, this book is not about Lewis's surprise, late-in-life marriage to Joy Davidman, whom he had not yet met at the time of his conversion.[1]

The apologetic from desire is a powerful apologetic for Christianity because it is difficult to argue against universal human feelings and desires. Only by prejudging the case and declaring that human desires are not worthy of study can one dismiss the important inner world of the person. Five thousand years of recorded history, on the other hand, chronicle in literature, the arts, and our scientific endeavors the depth of the human heart and mind. It is in literature and the arts that we find the human search for love, meaning, and virtuous behavior. We involve ourselves in art and math, not because these guarantee reproductive success in the natural scheme of things, but because of our deep longings to understand ourselves and our place in the universe. This is one reason why Christian schools want to be involved in the liberal arts. We want to gain knowledge from the sciences and the arts, not just to get better jobs, but to follow our desires for truth and wholeness and to relate better to our world and the God who created all that is. Our study in the liberal arts does not replace our need for Scripture but aids our

---

1. C. S. Lewis, *Surprised by Joy* (New York: Harcourt, Brace and World, 1955).

understanding of who God is, who we are, and what He expects of us in our world.

I HAVE A QUESTION

How do we know that these human desires aren't just a result of the need for food, or are submerged Freudian disappointments, or have some other explanation? Aren't we always reading in our textbooks about natural explanations for such things?

I cannot defend my position fully in this little box, but let me suggest that our academic textbooks do not have much evidence supporting such natural, biological explanations for our deep desires. What are often put forth are the shallow assumptions of the naturalistic worldview, which requires that everything about you have reductionistic explanations. Naturalism assumes that there is no deep nature to human beings; thus it concludes that deep human desires are the product of natural, animal, biological, genetic, or cultural forces. This is prejudging the case and never looking at alternative explanations.

As I previously suggested, one line of evidence to follow in this question is the incredible production and depth of human activity in the arts and sciences. The depth of human life far exceeds, and often moves in opposite directions to, basic survival motives. Read what comes next on these pages.

Cumulative Evidence

If someone asked me to prove beyond a shadow of doubt that the Christian worldview is true, I would have to answer that I could not do that. I would, however, suggest that if what is meant by the word *prove* is scientific proof, then we must admit that we cannot prove most of the things we hold most dear. Trivial matters or precisely defined, empirical realities seem to be the most open to proof by such means. But *prove* is never a word we can use with the most important and complex issues of life.

A woman cannot prove that she was in a certain shoe store today, and yet we may all agree that she was. How do we know beyond a shadow of doubt that she was present there during the ten o'clock hour? She could show us the cash register receipts for the shoes she bought there. We could search the chairs in the shoe store for elements of fabric or skin cells that would suggest her presence on that particular day. We could ask another store patron who sat in a neighboring chair whether she had seen the woman in that seat during that hour. What we are doing is collecting evidences from a variety of sources, including the woman's own testimony, and deciding in this case that she was, indeed, in that store sometime today. We believe because of the cumulative evidence we have collected.

Theistic reality is a complex subject matter that is not going to be shown to be true by one single line of evidence but by the accumulation of several types of evidence all pointing in the same direction. In the process we also may find evidences against the proposition that Christianity is true. This cumulative evidence process may mean examining historical and archaeological evidences, personal testimonies, prophecies in Scripture, and scientific credibility of biblical passages and answering objections such as those raised by the problem of suffering. When I was a nonbeliever, I made a search of many of the relevant evidences, and I found the case for Christianity to be solid enough for my belief. Since that time, I have been strengthened by many more evidences for the truth of Christianity.

The Question of Uncertainty

In this chapter on Christian evidences, I have to raise the question of whether it is okay to be less than 100 percent certain of our Christian beliefs. Many Christians feel that to be uncertain in matters of faith is equivalent to doubting God and lacking faith. Consequently, many Christian organizations have lengthy doctrinal statements about what is nonnegotiable in the Christian faith. Some Christian schools, on the other hand, have shocked certain churches or organizations because the schools' statements of faith are brief and do not contain references to abortion or evolution, for example. My college, Taylor University, along with many other Christian colleges, would explain that it is not that we do not have very conservative positions on such subjects but that we do not classify these topics among those things about which we are absolutely certain. This does not mean that faculty and staff are filled with doubts and weak faith about other things, but that they are open to examining certain positions with humility, knowing that they can always learn more about biblical content and the application of that content to the world.

Actually, some measure of uncertainty is a good indication of a well-tested and therefore, more secure faith. When a person is humble enough to admit that he or she does not know everything, then that person is open to new information and ideas. The universe is a large and complex place, not everything in the Bible is simple and easy to interpret and apply, and the ultimate truths about reality and personal experience are by no means easy to know. To say that biblical truth is void of any uncertainties does not answer the question of why there is frequent disagreement among good Christians on what the Bible teaches or what it means.

Humility of knowing should be the trademark of true knowledge. Knowledge comes because one realizes that one's perceptions must pass through a grid of personal opinions and feelings. Humility is the ability to admit that one does not know something or that there are evidences both against and in favor of one's position. Knowledge in this context can be expressed as percentages of certainty. For example, I might say, "I believe that abortion is wrong, but I do see some evidence against my position." One could take that to mean that I am 98 percent certain abortion is wrong according to the Bible, but I am also 2 percent uncertain because of particular arguments I have learned about.

If I have indeed examined the 2 percent of the evidence against my position, then I am more secure in what I hold, because I have seen arguments against my position and I continued in my belief. A stronger faith, not a weaker faith, results from such humility and openness to change. In some theological matters I may be more uncertain than in others. Who wrote the epistle to the Hebrews? Are the charismatic gifts valid today? For such questions I may be 60 percent certain and 40 percent uncertain or even 50-50 in my percentages. Low certainty percentages keep me studying, learning, and modifying my position, all of which make a path to a firmer knowledge.

In the past, when the church was dealing with issues for which there was a very high certainty on what the Scripture teaches, the church called such central beliefs dogma. We are almost absolutely certain the Bible teaches that God exists and that Jesus is His son. The decision in constructing a creed is to round off such strong, secure beliefs to 100 percent and say this is what we stand on as Christians. When, on the other hand, we claim absolute certainty for ideas for which we are not nearly as certain, we can be accused of being dogmatic. To be dogmatic about most matters in the Christian faith is not a good foundation for developing a strong faith. In fact, the opposite is the case. Dogmatism leads to indoctrination in teaching and not the entertaining of honest questions, and, in the long run, it weakens faith. Christian education should be committed to examining our faith, working on our uncertainties, and being willing to hold certain ideas in tension. In so doing we will be producing a stronger faith in our students.

I HAVE A QUESTION

But when does doubt or uncertainty become repulsive to God?

I hesitate to say that anything we do in our honest search for truth is repulsive to God. Jesus seemed to understand His disciples' honest mistakes and misunderstandings about Himself and His teachings. Uncertainty is not a bad thing, but an honest thing, a humble thing, a teach-me-because-I-know-so-little thing. Doubt, on the other hand, seems to be a refusal to believe, a refusal to search further to find the truth. Evidence can only take you so far on some issues, and then you have to go with it—to show faith in what you believe is correct. If there is sufficient evidence to merit your faith and you refuse to follow it for sinful or prideful reasons, then you doubt for reasons other than evidence.

SOME TERMS TO THINK ABOUT

apologetics. This word does not refer to apologizing. The Christian faith makes no apologies for its beliefs. The Christian worldview stands strong with evidence in the face of challenges. Apologetics means arguments or evidences, in this case, for the truth of the Christian worldview.

dogmatic. To act like you are 100 percent certain about something when the evidence is not that strong.

doubt. To refuse to go in the direction the evidence takes you. Thomas the apostle, whom we sometimes call "doubting Thomas," is probably unfairly labeled (John 20:24–29). When Thomas touched the hands and side of the risen Jesus Christ, he no longer doubted.

uncertainty. Having less than 100 percent certainty on a given subject. Christians ought to have some humility regarding their knowledge and certainty on many subjects in their faith.

FOURTEEN

A Christian View of Suffering

Somehow, pain and suffering were unleashed as necessary companions to misused human freedom. When man chose against God, his free world was forever spoiled.

PHILIP YANCEY

THE PROBLEM OF SUFFERING IS one of the most common objections to the Christian worldview. The problem stated briefly is as follows: Christians believe in an all-loving, all-powerful God. If God is all-loving, He would not want anyone to suffer. If God is all-powerful, then He would be able to prevent the suffering in people's lives. Since suffering still exists in the world, there must not be such a God. To be fair, this objection does not argue against the existence of God but only the Christian view of a God who is all-loving and all-powerful. The Muslim and the Jew do not necessarily have to believe that God is both all-loving and all-powerful. But given the New Testament picture of Jesus Christ working miracles of healing, Christians have no such choice.

The Christian answer to this problem of a good, all-powerful God and the presence of suffering in the world is framed very well in the second half of Romans 8. If I could paraphrase its first words, it says, "In the scales opposite human suffering is placed the grand

Epigraph. Philip Yancey, *Where Is God When It Hurts?* (Grand Rapids: Zondervan, 1977), 54.

purpose God has for human beings." The text reads: "I consider that our present sufferings are not worth comparing with the glory that will be revealed in us. The creation waits in eager expectation for the sons of God to be revealed" (Rom. 8:18–19).

If the enormity of human suffering is somehow to be seen as "worth it," then God's purpose for human beings, under which all suffering is permitted, must be truly outstanding. And, indeed, God's purpose for human beings is amazing to say the least. In an earlier chapter of this book, I wrote about human purpose being to give glory to God, which means to reveal who God is, not just with our words and worship, but with every aspect of our lives, now and for eternity.

This glorious purpose for human beings was revealed during God's creation of Adam and Eve, by what might be called the theology of "creation in harm's way." One question concerning the Genesis account of creation is why God created Adam and Eve in danger's way? Why did God create His prized humanity in a place to which Satan had access? Why did God not first rid the world of Satan and his demons or create Adam and Eve somewhere else?

The answer to these questions is that God obviously intended to create Adam and Eve in harm's way. But why? The answer begins in Genesis 1:26–28, which states that mankind was created in God's image and then told to rule the earth. God created a being in His image and then gave that being God's work to do. It is almost as if God stepped back and said, "You, mankind, are to end the angelic conflict. You are to bring love into this world. I could do it, but I want you to do that job." God wants us to do His works and thus reveal His character and purposes. This is what it means to give glory to God, to reveal His nature and character.

For God to step back and let us do His work means that there is a chance we will fail God and commit sins in the process. In fact, that did happen and continues to happen because of the fall of Adam and Eve. But God values our freedom and His purpose for us more than He values immediately eliminating the horrors of sin and suffering. He must understand far more than we the anguish of sins and suffering because of His perspective on the Cross.

It is not as if God left humanity on its own to do His work in a dangerous world. Genesis 3:15 suggests that God Himself would enter the world as a human being. The God of the universe would work as the head of the human race to defeat evil and end the angelic rebellion. In the New Testament, Jesus, God the Son, tells His disciples that He is leaving the church age responsibilities up to them, but He will send the Holy Spirit to indwell and empower them. I am sure the disciples were thinking, "Why doesn't Jesus remain here? He could do a better job with the gospel message than we could. We will sin, and we will suffer."

If God wanted to end all human sin and suffering, all He would have to do is to return today and usher in eternity. But God the Son has not returned. And every day that He does not return, more sins and sufferings occur. God obviously values humanity's opportunities to act like God, in His place, more than He wants at this moment to remove the sins and suffering of the world. And all this discussion of God's willingness to permit sins and suffering must be put into the context of the fact that He will one day bring an end to this drama of Christians living like Christ in a world of sin and suffering.

I HAVE A QUESTION

You just left me behind in all this. What is "creation in harm's way," and how does it relate to this chapter on suffering?

Creation in harm's way means that God created human beings in danger's way, that is, on planet Earth, where Satan was free to tempt them. How could God make such a mistake, which would lead to sin and suffering of unbelievable proportions? It was no mistake. God, from the very beginning, created human beings in His image in order that they might glorify Him and do His work on earth and in the universe for all eternity. God saw that special purpose for human beings as more important in the long run than creating a world where there could be no suffering.

Since sins and suffering are unbelievably numerous and horrendous, and have been for thousands of years, how great His purpose in human beings must be! Your purpose in life is not just to have babies or go to church but to reveal the nature and character of God for all eternity. Suffering and sins will be done away with some day, and the eternal day for which we were all created will begin. But no less important are the days we spend on earth today, where sins and suffering abound. During this day of potential sin and suffering, we are to choose to exhibit God's character of love.

This choice for human freedom and the consequent risk of sin and suffering that God made is not so foreign to human thinking. Most of us make the same decision when we choose to seek relationships with others. To love means to risk being hurt. Would we not all choose to marry and love deeply for twenty years and then have a spouse die, rather than never love anyone and, therefore, never be hurt? The saying, "Better to have loved and lost than never to have loved at all," seems true. The suffering that we are going through now is little when weighed in the scales opposite the possibility of our glorifying God and entering a love relationship with Him and each other.

God creates human beings and asks them to do His work in His place and to love and live for all eternity showing His nature and love. God voluntarily limits Himself by creating free creatures in order to bring those who will into a love relationship with Himself. In other words, in spite of the pain, it is worth it to be human beings who are loved by God and enter into a love relationship with Him and with each other.

Let me return to those often-quoted verses in Romans 8 to restate this view of suffering that exists in a world controlled by an all-powerful, all-loving God, who has a wonderful purpose for human beings. We are to be His children, in His image, and exist in love relationships for all eternity. In times of suffering, we are asked by a loving God to believe that all these hard times are worth the amazing love and life He has prepared for us. "I consider that our present sufferings are not worth comparing with the glory that will be revealed in us. The creation waits in eager expectation for the sons of God to be revealed. For the creation was subjected to frustration, not by its own choice, but by the will of the one who subjected it, in hope that the creation itself will be liberated from its bondage to decay and brought into the glorious freedom of the children of God. . . . And we know that in all things God works for the good of those who love him, who have been called according to his purpose" (Rom. 8:18–21, 28).

I HAVE A QUESTION

Somehow I just don't feel that higher purpose in my life when I am in Christian churches. All I feel is that I am guilty and bad and ought to clean up my act or face certain punishment. Why do Christian churches not make me feel good about myself if this is all true?

Churches are in the difficult position of having to gather sinners in and help them to mature spiritually. This means talking about sins and at the same time talking about God's love for them. The religious Pharisees in Jesus' day made the mistake of pushing sinners aside while promoting their own self-righteousness and forgetting about the love God wanted to show to all human beings. Every church needs to learn to use the message of God's love as motivation for spiritual growth and to not use guilt feelings to motivate the masses in the pews.

By the way, the Christian message is about truth and not about feeling good. We do commit sins, and we need to change. That truth does not "feel good." But the truth that God loves us no matter what is what should motivate us to seek His new life and His help in transforming us into images of His Son, Jesus Christ.

Finding Meaning in Life in Spite of Suffering

At some time in their lives, most human beings will ask, "What is my life all about? What is the ultimate meaning of my accomplishments, of my failures, of my suffering?" In answering these questions, it is important to have a clear definition of the phrase "meaning in life." Meaning in anything relates to connectedness. To give a student a Q on his report card is meaningless, not that the student does not know what a Q is, but that he does not know what meaningful performance standard a Q is connected to. Is a Q a bad grade or not? We cannot know until we connect it to a grade description, such as Q = excellent. An F grade, on the other hand, is meaningful. We connect 50 percent to an F, which means failure, which is connected to not passing a course, which is connected to not graduating from college, and so on. If one of our parents suffers a fatal heart attack, it means something to us because we connect the heart attack to the loss of a loved one, financial insecurity, or fears for our own mortality.

The reason there is no meaning to life in atheistic or pantheistic worldviews is because the events in one's life do not connect to any larger picture of reality. There is no plot or story or message to the universe. A book with a random assignment of letters over the pages is meaningless. And the same is true of a book composed of a single letter repeated on every page. The pieces never add up to anything. To the atheist there is only evolving bits of matter. There cannot be greater values given to some arrangements than to others. There is no purpose or ultimate value arising from suffering. In pantheism the question of meaning in life and suffering is even murkier than in atheism. The wholeness and oneness of all contains no possibility of even random pattern or design. All complexity and pattern is an illusion. Christians understand that meaning can only exist in a connected message or story, and ultimately only in a Story Maker.

The Christian view of reality says that God exists and has a design and purpose for the universe and human life. The individual events and choices of our lives, including our sufferings, fit into a larger scheme of things. Ecclesiastes 3:1–8 is perhaps the most poetic expression in the Bible of the existence of meaning in God's universe. These well-known verses suggest that we ought to see life as a time line that contains both good and bad events, good times and suffering times. "There is … a time to be born and a time to die," and so on for seven more verses. Meaning in life, according to Ecclesiastes 3:1–8, does not come because someone has minimal or no suffering but because God exists, and even one's suffering fits into a larger picture and purpose.

Put into a more modern form, the message of Ecclesiastes 3 is that there is no meaning in a single frame of a motion picture or one page of a long novel. If we were to see a single, one-twenty-fourth-second picture frame in a movie, and it showed a man and a woman driving a car off a steep cliff, what would this scene mean to us? That picture would mean nothing. We want to know who they are. Are they the good or the bad characters in the story? What is the story that leads to their driving off a cliff? The entire film—the plot, characters, and action—gives meaning to the individual frames. If we learn that the couple driving off the cliff are just characters in a dream, it means something different to us than if we discover they are the hero and the heroine. The overall story gives meaning to the second-by-second details.

Christianity says that life is not a series of disconnected moments but is a whole story and our lives and sufferings fit into the whole of the drama in an important way. At this moment we can see our moments of suffering only from a limited perspective, and, like Job, who suffered much and was not told why, we are asked to trust God that there is meaning to our moments of suffering. Our limited time on earth is connected to a larger plot and design for human life, and we ourselves are connected meaningfully to a God who loves us and invites us into His family and story.

In the actual moments of suffering, people do not need a quote from Ecclesiastes 3 to make them feel better about cancer or death. What they need is an understanding, loving arm around their shoulders. And all of us need ingrained into our minds that when suffering occurs, there is a larger story within which God's love is protecting and guarding our lives. We may not see that larger story from where we stand at the funeral or in the hospital bed, but we are asked to believe in that God who wrote our story into His.

SOME TERMS TO THINK ABOUT

creation in harm's way. An explanation for why God allows suffering. God created free human beings who could love and "act like God" in the world. But those human beings could also choose to glorify themselves instead of God and thus increase suffering in the world.

meaning. Many connected parts making a whole, meaningful picture. All things fit into a larger scheme of things. Meaningful things fit into a larger plan. Christians believe in meaning in life because God has a plan for us and orchestrates this plan alongside human choice.

suffering. Christians believe that suffering is real and not an illusion. They believe that every human being will suffer physically and emotionally. The suffering of animals is debatable to some, but that hardly changes the view of a suffering world under God.

FIFTEEN

Living the Christian Worldview in the World

A many-sided debate about the relations of Christianity and civilization is being carried on in our time. . . . It is carried on publicly by opposing parties and privately in the conflicts of conscience. Sometimes it is concentrated on special issues, such as those of the place of Christian faith in general education or of Christian ethics in economic life. Sometimes it deals with broad questions of the church's responsibility for social order or of the need for a new separation of Christ's followers from the world.

H. RICHARD NIEBUHR

THE IDEAS IN THIS BOOK COULD be read and discussed in classrooms, homes, and churches, but it is when worldviews are lived out that they change what is happening in people's lives. Worldview beliefs do affect one's life and culture, so it is important to consider how the Christian worldview should be lived out and affect our society. The heart of good integration of faith and learning is the eventual presence of a Christian faith that can be salt and light to a world that needs plenty of both. Unfortunately, Christian theism

---

Epigraph. H. Richard Niebuhr, *Christ and Culture* (New York: Harper and Row, 1951), 1.

often exists only in churches or seminary classrooms as opposed to the "streets" of our lives and cultures.

Sacred-Versus-Secular Division

A long-standing issue in the Christian faith is the sacred-versus-secular debate. This debate arises from the tendency of Christians to divide the world of human thought and behavior into two parts, the sacred and the secular. The sacred refers to religious and holy things, thoughts, and behaviors. The secular refers to everything else, whether sinful or not. Any sacred-secular division has consequences in an educational arena like a Christian college. Biblical subjects can be seen as more important or more spiritual than other subjects such as the sciences or the arts. And certain college activities, such as sports, films, non-Christian music events, and science and political lectures, may be seen as less important and certainly less holy than evangelistic programs.

The reasons for a sacred-secular division of ideas and behaviors are many, but they often come down to a few strong opinions. Sometimes the division arises because of an overemphasis on the "sacred mission" of the church, which is the evangelization of the world. Every other human endeavor is seen as being of secondary importance when compared to the work of saving souls from eternal damnation. Sacred-secular splits also occur because of secular behavior or teachings that Christians find particularly offensive. These often occur in areas like psychology, literature, film, and the other arts. "Why spend your time studying subjects where sin and error abound?" many Christians ask. Sometimes the sacred-secular division arises from a call to higher holiness, somewhat like the monastic movements of the past. "Separate yourself from the world and its sins," becomes the message.

One argument against separating the sacred from the secular is that Christians have not just been given the Great Commission of evangelism in Matthew 28, but also a cultural mandate beginning in the book of Genesis. Christians may not be *of* the world, but they can still be *in* the world, relating as salt and light to the world's culture and knowledge pursuits. The question is whether we should withdraw from the world to protect our purity, or whether we should enter the world to help change it with our world and life view. It may also be true that those who favor a sacred-secular division fear the possibility of sin more than they value the richness of human nature and all God's creation. God, in whose image we were created, is wise and creative, as well as righteous. God created nature beautiful and understandable, and He created us with the capability to know and to create. All of this is to say that the Great Commission is larger than evangelism and that God's work through us means developing human beings in moral, social, intellectual, and aesthetic ways after the image of their Creator.

Those who favor a sacred-secular split say that we should not waste time on things that are not of eternal value. However, we must remember that it is not religious activities that are of eternal value but the persons who embrace them. It is our personhood in God's image that is of eternal value, and whatever contributes to our personhood has eternal significance. True religion is not found in religious activities alone but in anything that unifies human thought and behavior with God. In a Christian liberal arts college, we see sacredness in the science class, the intramural programs, the violin lessons, and the international study trip, as well as in biblical studies, chapel programs, and mission activities. We Christians should seek Christ's redemptive work in every facet of our personhood and our world.

I HAVE A QUESTION

But don't you think that there are some things or many things that we Christians cannot associate ourselves with? And aren't some people particularly sensitive to or tempted by some evils and secular situations in the world? Don't we need to create an environment that protects them? The Scriptures do say to protect our "weaker brother."

You ask a couple of good questions for this small box. Let me answer yes in principle to your questions. Yes, there are certainly things and sins in the world that everyone, not just Christians, ought to avoid. The questions usually arise over what those things are. A good example of that type of question is whether a Christian should attend R-rated movies. Yes, some people are weaker and more prone to sin in certain situations than other people. As a result we may have different standards, but as you have indicated, we who have liberties in some areas need to make sure we do not hurt the faith of those who do not have those freedoms.

All Christians would admit that age plays a factor in these questions. There are many things that children should not be allowed to do, and they certainly should be given protection against some of the dangers in the world. That fact alone, however, does not tell us what schools to send our children to. Very few issues in Christian living are as simple as saying no to the things of the world. And the best protection for young people may not be to withdraw them from culture but to teach them how to live in the world without being captured by it.

Changing Human Nature

In Aldous Huxley's *Brave New World,* we have examples of assumptions about human nature that are applied to the real world of human problems. In Huxley's novel people are seen as the products of genetic engineering and early-life conditioning. Therefore, human problems are solved simply by engineering a more perfect genetic product. Also, conditioning and sleep teaching are applied to the minds of children in order to create the proper emotions and patterns of thought. It is presuppositions about the physical nature of human beings in *Brave New World* that lead to attempts to solve every human problem by biological or conditioning strategies.[1]

We do not live in the brave new world, but the naturalistic

---

1. Aldous Huxley, *Brave New World* (1969; repr., New York: Harper Collins, 1998).

worldview of our age is beginning to move in that direction. Our predominant cultural worldview may not usually be atheistic, but it does favor the assumption that human problems can best be solved by designer drugs and genetic engineering. Also, our current culture tends to believe that if a behavior, such as homosexuality, has biological or genetic predispositions, it must be okay. It is almost as if we are losing hope that things will ever get better for humanity, unless some radical biological discoveries are made that will solve all of our medical, personal, and social problems. That was the hope and purpose of the brave new world experiment.

Another philosophical segment of our culture, secular humanism, sees the inner potential of a human being as sufficient to solve all of humanity's problems. This humanistic viewpoint is at odds with the Christian view of the sin nature when it suggests that people are naturally directed toward the good and the perfect. The goal of secular humanism is to remove the restrictions and commandments that tend to squash the human potential to change for the better. Thus, a society seen as too permissive by those of a religious bent is seen as liberating by those of the human potential movement. The reason our culture is turning its attention toward genetic engineering as a cure for human problems is because the human potential movement, with its own brand of moral relativism, has not produced the perfect world. In fact, one could argue that in the absence of rules and restraints, the worst of human nature often emerges.

The Christian should not completely reject biological or human potential solutions to human problems. The Christian worldview can accept that we are bodies with physical natures and that we have great potential to be more than we are. What the Christian worldview insists on is that we are more than mere biology, and biological solutions by themselves will leave us short of a perfect personality and world. Also, while human beings have great abilities to rise above their limitations, human potential is restricted by a broken, sinful human nature.

The facts of human sin nature and the human need for spiritual life should be the impetus behind the sharing of the gospel of Jesus Christ. The Christian gospel of forgiveness of sins and a relationship with Jesus Christ, the God of the universe, is exactly what is needed to repair our world and its people. That gospel must be worked out into society, not just by preaching from the pulpits, but also by the ideas and behaviors seen in Christians as they enter every segment of society.

Interacting with the Worldviews of the World

The worldviews that we encounter in the world are not usually exact copies of those we have learned about in this book. Rather, they are livable versions of the classic worldviews. In textbooks we learn about atheism and pantheism. But in real life, on the street, in the next-door neighbor, in the friend at work, we will rarely see these worldviews lived out in their classic forms. There are two reasons for this. First, unlike Christian theism, other worldviews have major flaws in their description of the human person with regard to purpose and value, and thus they are nearly impossible to live out in daily life. Second, the average person on the street is not academically searching for a worldview to base life upon; he or she simply absorbs a worldview or parts of several worldviews from the surrounding culture.

Therefore, on the streets we are most likely to meet a secular humanist, whose worldview is an altered form of atheistic naturalism. Secular humanism assigns value and purpose to a human being against all reason, even though the universe is materialistic and void of God. Relativism (self-determination of right and wrong) becomes the cultural norm. We are also likely to meet a person in the New Age movement, whose "faith" is an altered form of pantheism. Pantheism denies the existence of personhood or any discrete, physical reality. The New Age movement allows one to still be real, along with his new car and girlfriend. Future spiritual growth into a being of power happens in mysterious ways—maybe through meditation, hallucinogenic drugs, or even crystal and pyramid power in one's furniture.

I used to believe that showing the lack of evidence for, or the illogical conclusions resulting from, such views on the street was the way to show people the truth of Christian theism. I still believe we have to begin by knowing intellectually the foundation on which we stand and being able to see the flaws in other choices. But we cannot stop there. The person on the street or in the office next door is no longer thinking rationally about his or her choice of belief or behavior. The person may not even be aware that he or she has a worldview, let alone an illogical one. Many people have patched together versions of two or three worldviews in order to make their choice of lifestyle livable.

Wrong worldviews, or erroneous distortions of the Christian worldview, will eventually disrupt a person's life and happiness. It is at the point of daily living that we must confront other worldviews with the living out of our own beliefs. We should live with love for our neighbors, a commitment for values, and a sense of purpose, and be a calming influence during times of storm. Then the world of neighbor and friend takes note and digs deeper into the reason for our hope and Christlike character.

I HAVE A QUESTION

I have learned a lot, honestly, but are we done yet?

Yes, you have been exposed to a lot of ideas, and we are finished. Thanks for paying attention. Take a look at the books in the "For Further Reading" list. These are all "classic" books that a thinking Christian ought to read sometime. Now go out and see how these ideas work in the real world!

SOME TERMS TO THINK ABOUT

Brave New World. A science fiction novel by Aldous Huxley that was way ahead of its time. Published in 1932 it forecasts an earth nearly united under the control of a naturalistic worldview and the science of genetic engineering. Huxley, by the way, was warning us of such a world, and he would be disappointed to know that many of his predictions have come to pass.[2]

cultural mandate. The command of God to Adam and Eve and all their descendants to be stewards of this world (Gen. 1:26–28).

Great Commission. The command of Jesus Christ to spread the gospel of salvation to the entire world and to disciple those who believe (Matt. 28:18–20).

sacred versus secular. Holy versus less holy; spiritual versus sinful; church attendance versus playing golf on Sunday; playing the organ in church versus French horn in the school band; Paul of Tarsus versus Shakespeare; reading Psalm 51 versus reading a commentary on Psalm 51; the pope saying Mass versus Brother Lawrence washing dishes.

---

2. Ibid., xvii.

For Further Reading

Of making many books there is no end, and much study wearies the body. (Ecclesiastes 12:12b)

THE TEACHER

I HAVE PURPOSELY KEPT THIS reading list brief in the hope that interested readers will pursue a few of the key books on the topics of faith and learning, worldviews, and Christian theism. A longer reading list, I fear, might discourage further reading, or worse, might weary both the mind and the body. Each of these books provided a title quote for one of the chapters in this book. Most of these books are modern classics that are well worth reading in spite of busy schedules.

Abbott, Edwin A. *Flatland: A Romance of Many Dimensions*. New York: Barnes and Noble, 1963.

This classic book on a topic in mathematics was written by a Victorian scholar in theology and literature. This story about a two-dimensional world discovering the reality of another dimension shows up repeatedly in pastors' sermons. The lesson it teaches is what Christians and New Age believers teach. The natural realm is not all there is, for a spiritual realm exists around us. This spiritual dimension is no less real simply because it is unseen.

Barcus, Nancy B. *Developing a Christian Mind*. Downers Grove, Ill.: InterVarsity, 1977.

> This gem was written by an assistant professor of English at Houghton College and reads with ease and clarity through difficult ideas. We ought to read more books by English professors. If they have something to say, they usually know how to say it.

Camus, Albert. *The Stranger*. New York: Vintage Books, 1942.

> This is a well-written book by a famous atheistic existentialist and Nobel Prize winner in literature. The book's main character, Meursault, lives life the way an honest-to-his-assumptions atheistic existentialist would. This book has one of the most famous first lines in a book, as Meursault expresses little or no emotions about his mother's death.

Gaebelein, Frank E. *The Pattern of God's Truth*. Chicago: Moody, 1954.

> This scholar and educator wrote on Christian education from his thirty years of experience as headmaster at Stony Brook School, one of America's finest college preparatory schools. He was also coeditor of *Christianity Today* magazine. I was a guest lecturer at Stony Brook years ago, and I was thoroughly impressed with their teachers and students.

Harris, Robert A. *The Integration of Faith and Learning: A Worldview Approach*. Eugene, Ore.: Cascade Books, 2004.

> A well-written book by a college teacher of writing, literature, and critical thinking for more than twenty-five years. Critical thinking skills are a forgotten subject in our schools today, but Robert Harris uses them well in this book.

Holmes, Arthur F. *All Truth Is God's Truth*. Grand Rapids: Eerdmans, 1977.

> This Christian philosopher and Wheaton College professor has written some of the best books published on faith and learning

and the merits of Christian education. When I interviewed for my first college teaching appointment, I interviewed at two excellent colleges, Wheaton and Taylor. I remember hearing that every interviewee at Wheaton College had to meet with Arthur Holmes in order to show competence in faith and learning issues. Apparently one had to pass through his gate in order to be seriously considered for a faculty position at Wheaton. Arthur Holmes asked me faith-and-learning questions in my twenty minutes with him. I gave my answers and passed the test, but in that short time I learned much from him as well.

Kreeft, Peter. *Between Heaven and Hell.* Downers Grove, Ill.: InterVarsity, 1982.

Several fascinating books have come from Peter Kreeft, who teaches on philosophical and Christian topics by creating marvelous characters who debate the issues. In this book John F. Kennedy, Aldous Huxley, and C. S. Lewis, each of whom died on November 22, 1963, meet after death and debate what might come next. Another one of Kreeft's books written in the same style and well worth reading is *The Unaborted Socrates.*

Lewis, C. S. *Mere Christianity.* New York: Macmillan, 1943.

This famous Oxford professor wrote some of the best and clearest books in defense of and explanation of the Christian faith. This book is worth reading many times, since more can be gleaned each time it is read. Follow up *Mere Christianity*'s explanation of what Christians believe with Lewis's science fiction trilogy, beginning with *Out of the Silent Planet*, and you will see a living version of what Christians believe.

Little, Paul E. *Know Why You Believe.* 4th edition. Downers Grove, Ill.: InterVarsity, 2000.

This is a classic book still in Christian bookstores years after its initial publication, and for good reason. Paul Little gives clear answers to the dozen most common objections to the Christian faith.

This book is a small, powerful book to give to people who are interested in the Christian faith but wonder about some of the common objections to Christianity. I was just such a person in graduate school, and this book answered my objections. Remember, however, that all the evidence in the world, no matter how good, will not necessarily convince a person to believe in Christianity. The first prerequisite to belief in anything is a willingness to believe.

Mackay, Donald M. *The Clock Work Image.* Downers Grove, Ill.: InterVarsity, 1974.

In this modern classic, Mackay, who is both a scientist and a Christian, writes about the reality of the natural law within the supernatural realm of the Christian. His approach to faith-and-learning integration defends the idea that Christians can embrace the natural sciences without reducing human nature to mere mechanism.

Nash, Ronald H. *Worldviews in Conflict.* Grand Rapids: Zondervan, 1992.

This author and philosophy teacher at a leading seminary examines and tests the Christian worldview. Since so many good books come from Christians with philosophy degrees, we all would be wise to study more in that arena of thought.

Naugle, David K. *Worldview: The History of a Concept.* Grand Rapids: Eerdmans, 2002.

This is a large book with everything you ever wanted to know about worldviews. It is a tough read but well worth having on your library shelf. David Naugle is a professor of philosophy at Dallas Baptist University. I guest lectured at this excellent Christian college years ago, and my topic was on the Christian view of the brain and determinism. There was a hearing-impaired young woman in the class. She sat in the front row, and her interpreter sat to the front and side of her. I even now remember using big words like "amygdala" and "hippocampus," and thinking how much effort that young woman and her interpreter were putting into every class she was taking. From that moment on, I tried to lecture and write more with my audience in mind.

Niebuhr, H. Richard. *Christ and Culture.* New York: Harper and Row, 1951.

This classic book gives five basic ways of relating Christ and culture, or faith and learning. Niebuhr's ideas are still in use today, even if we give them other labels.

Schaeffer, Francis A. *Escape from Reason.* Downers Grove, Ill.: InterVarsity, 1968.

This was one of the initial books in modern Christian thought literature from the founder of L' Abri Fellowship in Switzerland. Francis Schaeffer and his many books provided the early soil in which a generation of Christian thinkers, including myself, were nurtured. Francis Schaeffer did not just write books and travel the lecture circuit. He carried a passion for the truth and for Christians learning it and applying it. Francis Schaeffer lectured at Taylor University for one of his last speaking engagements. I still today remember this weak, dying Christian man in Swiss knickers retreating, after his talk, to the ambulance that waited for him outside the auditorium.

Shakespeare, William. *Hamlet.* New York: Penguin, 1980.

Hamlet was a man who saw life with passion and morality, unlike Meursault of *The Stranger.* I could not pass up the chance to show their opposite opening thoughts on the death of a parent. These opening thoughts are examples of thinking with the atheistic existentialist mind-set in the bland character of Meursault versus thinking with a Christian theistic mind-set in the passionate character of Hamlet. One worthwhile movie version of this Shakespearean masterpiece stars Mel Gibson as Hamlet. It is amazingly good and not just a *Lethal Weapon* meets *Hamlet.*

Sire, James W. *The Universe Next Door*. 3d edition. Downers Grove, Ill.: InterVarsity, 1997.

James Sire, former Wheaton literature professor and editor of InterVarsity Press, has written one of the best and most popular books on worldview in the last twenty-five years. This book was an early contributor to my education on faith and learning. I met Jim Sire years ago at InterVarsity Press when I was looking for a publisher for one of my books. I was impressed with him then and continue to be impressed with his latest books.

Trueblood, D. Elton. *Philosophy of Religion*. Grand Rapids: Baker, 1973.

This former Stanford and later Earlham professor wrote with unusual clarity about complicated philosophical ideas important to Christian thinkers. He was such an influential thinker and teacher at Earlham College in Indiana that a library about the size of a small house was built just for him. In the comfort of his books, Elton Trueblood chatted year after year with eager college students wanting to learn from a "legend."

Yancey, Philip. *Where Is God When It Hurts?* Grand Rapids: Zondervan, 1977.

It is hard to find a better modern writer today on issues of suffering and faith than Philip Yancey. He is a multiple award-winning writer with a gift for making us all think and see more inside of the tough issues like suffering. Years ago Phil Yancey (with Paul Brand) wrote a book on the human body *(Fearfully and Wonderfully Made),* and so did I. His book sold millions, and mine just sold. It is easy to be humble in the presence of this gifted writer and speaker.

Author and Subject Index

absolute truth, 24, 96
absurdity, 109, 111–12, 114–15
Adam and Eve, 145–47, 168
anthropological crisis, 95, 97
anthropology, 30, 34
anti-intellectualism, 40, 51–52
apologetic from desire, 160–62
apologetics, 157–58, 166
assumptions. *See* presuppositions
atheism, 68, 105. *See also* atheistic
naturalism; atheistic
existentialism
atheistic existentialism, 69, 81, 108–11,
172; and atheistic naturalism,
108; testing the evidence for,
112; testing the existential
repugnance of, 113; testing the
logical consistency of, 112–13;
value and meaning in, 113–14;
view of God, 112; view of human
nature, 109, 111–13, 117
atheistic naturalism, 76, 85–86,
88, 95–99, 127, 131, 179–80;
compared to secular humanism,
98–99; ethics in, 91–92; testing
the evidence for, 92–93; testing
the existential repugnance of, 94;
testing the logical consistency
of, 93–94; origins of, 85, 95;
understanding of human nature,
87–90, 92–93, 99, 162; view of
human nature, 68–69, 140–41.
See also epistemological crisis,

the; anthropological crisis, the;
reductionism
Atman, 119–21, 123

Bible, the, 26, 36–37, 56–57, 140–43,
146–48, 173; contribution to
knowledge, 38–39, 44–45,
55; human limitations of
understanding, 47; view of sin,
144 (*see also* human nature; sin).
See also Christian theism
Brahman, 119–21, 123, 126
Brave New World (Huxley), 178, 182
Buddhism, 117, 120

Camus, Albert, *The Stranger*, 113
Cartesian dualism, 86
Christ. *See* Jesus of Nazareth (Christ)
Christian theism, 34, 68, 75–76, 100,
134, 137–38, 171; compared
to the New Age movement,
129–30, 132; explanation for
human desires, 138, 160–62;
and logic, 104; objections
to, 135–36, 158–65, 167; as
postmodern viewpoint, 82; and
sacred versus secular debate,
176, 182; and suffering, 167–74;
testing the evidence for, 138–39,
157–66; testing the existential
repugnance of, 139; testing the
logical consistency of, 139; view
of human nature, 111–12,

189